Prayer:
A Force
that Causes
Change

Time to Pray
VOLUME 5

DAVID WILLIAMSON

Trafford
PUBLISHING

 www.trafford.com

North America & international
toll-free: 1 888 232 4444 (USA & Canada)
phone: 250 383 6864 ♦ fax: 812 355 4082

DEDICATION

This book is dedicated to men and women of effective, fervent prayer. You teach success in prayer by example, and inspire and encourage, running the race to be the best. Thank you for your demonstration of faith, love and the power of Christ, and your wonderful prayers.

TABLE OF CONTENTS

Introduction: A Call to the Team   ix

Unit One   **Empowered for Prayer**   1

     Article 1   The Fallow Ground   5

     Article 2   Revelations   11

     Article 3   More Revelations   19

     Article 4   The Stumble   27

     Article 5   Who Do You Say I Am?   35

     Article 6   Light   41

     Article 7   Twisted Thinking   47

     Article 8   In The Neighborhood   53

     Article 9   Character And Prayer   59

Unit Two   **Passion For Effective Prayer**   65

     Article 10   Up To . . .   69

     Article 11   I Am . . .   75

     Article 12   Taking Our Place   83

     Article 13   Like Eagles   91

     Article 14   Partners   97

     Article 15   3 Days Before Answers   103

     Article 16   Facing The Granite Wall   109

     Article 17   Razor Sharp   115

     Article 18   The Best   119

Unit Three   **Time for Prayer**   123

     Article 19   Open Doors   127

     Article 20   Closed Doors   135

     Article 21   Good Government   141

Article 22   The City of our GoD   147

Article 23   Breakup the Fallow Ground   151

Article 24   The List   155

Article 25   Go In and Possess   161

Prayer For Salvation   167

A Few Selected Books on Prayer   169

The Book Series and Newsletter   171

Introduction

A CALL TO THE TEAM

When I was growing up I loved baseball; I loved both playing and watching. Summers were filled with baseball, baseball, and baseball. Some days I played organized ball on a team in the city league for boys my age. However, this was not enough baseball for me, so most afternoons we played pick-up games.

A pick-up game begins with a ritual that is as old as the game itself. Two boys are captains of the teams and pick their teammates. One captain would pick and then the other captain would pick. They alternate back and forth, until everyone was on a team. Then we played ball.

And what about you, have you been picked? The Father is picking people and He wants everyone on His team. Unfortunately, some people do not respond to being picking. When He points to them and says "come," inviting them to be on His team, they are too busy or not interested. Beyond being picked to be on the team, the Father is also calling people to specific assignments in the Body of Christ.

Using my baseball example, you are picked to be on the team and then you are assigned to play a position, such as playing at third base. There are, as mentioned above, people who choose not to be picked for the team. There are also people who have responded to being picked, but have not responded by taking their assigned position on the team.

Have you ever seen the Lipizzaner Stallions? These magnificent horses have performed their shows of beauty and skill to millions of people around the world? These animals are amazing and able to do things far beyond what most of us imagine horses can do. These horses are doing what they were created to do and doing it very well.

Sometimes people do not do what they are created to do. And not doing what God has called them to do, it is like a horse with all the correct blood lines to be a Lipizzaner Stallion, being a plow horse. Now I do not mean to offend you, if you or someone you love is a plow horse. There is nothing wrong with being a plow horse, it is a noble profession, but it is not a good thing to be, if you are called to be a Lipizzaner Stallion.

You have been picked to be on the greatest team of all time, the Body of Christ. And beyond this, the Father has assigned you to a special role on the team. It is vitally important to the team and to your health and happiness, that you join the team and do your assigned part. Not doing what you are called to do is like being a plow horse when you are called to be a Lipizzaner.

Beyond that, there are people who are in their place, but they have not sought to fulfill the high calling of God. They are satisfied to wander through life, while picked and in place, they are doing less than their God enabled best. It is like being a Lipizzaner Stallion, but just hanging around the barn, never preparing and going to the arena for your performance.

Where do you stand today? Have you responded to the Father? Have you said yes to salvation in Christ Jesus; repented of your sin, believed in your heart, and confessed with your mouth that Jesus is Lord?

Have you sought to hear from the Father and responded to His call. Are you taking your place in the Body of Christ and have you taken the position that He assigned? And are you working with the Holy Spirit to fulfill all the Father has called you to do?

Our responding to His call is very important. Please do not feel condemned about this, His invitation to salvation is open to all, His call is unique to you, and His empowerment for service is geared for you, the need, and His perfect timing. But the question is have you responded?

We always thank God for all of you as we remember you in our prayers. In the presence of our God and Father, we never forget that your faith is active, your love is working hard, and your confidence in our Lord Jesus Christ is enduring. Brothers and sisters, we never forget this because we know that God loves you and has chosen you.

1 Thessalonians 1:2-4 (God's Word)

Paul writes to the Thessalonians, and we would be wise to read his words just as if the letter was addressed to us. He expresses his thankfulness for us. He is pleased that we are active in faith, working hard in love, and have confidence in Jesus. He is pleased that our efforts for the team continue. Note his declaration, God so love us that He picked us for His team. And He has chosen us for specific assignments.

In any assignment it is easy to slip into something less than the Father's best and fullness. We can grow weary, we can get busy, and we can become satisfied with where we are or what we have to do. There are many dangers we can slip into, this is true in all kinds of assignments and seen in many places. Notice the report on the church in Ephesus. They were working, but they had begun to slip.

I know your works, your labor, your patience, and that you cannot bear those who are evil. And you have tested those who say they are apostles and are not, and have found them liars; and you have persevered and have patience, and have labored for My name's sake and have not become weary. Nevertheless I have this against you, that you have left your first love. Remember therefore

from where you have fallen; repent and do the first
works, or else I will come to you quickly and remove
your lampstand from its place—unless you repent.

REVELATION 2:2-5 (NKJV)

Here the Lord is focusing on their first works, but this warning is just as valid for us; we should be seeking to fulfill all He has called us to do. In prayer there is praying for our daily need and desires, and also praying for the needs of other people, ministries, and even for nations. Some people slipped away from Gods call and do not pray. Some people pray, but it is only as duty and dismissed without much thought or expectation. However, God is looking for people who will pray; believing God's word and having faith that He can and will do all He has promised.

God has offered us the noble position of prayer. He is looking for men and women who will rise up and fulfill His calling; who will pray effective, fervent prayers that avail much. It is time to pray!

The world around us is racing to its destruction. Descriptions of the horrors of the Last Days are now daily readings in the newspapers. And yet, God's promise of an outpouring of His Spirit has not passed away. God's promise of the power and effectiveness of prayer has not ended or been cast aside. The only question is, will God find a man or woman, or several, who will believe that the days of His power, are not over and that He can and will bring great and wonderful answers to prayers? Will He find a man or woman, laboring fervently for people, churches, cities, and nations? Will He find men and women of powerful, effective, prayer? How about you?

The great outpourings of God have begun in desperate times, when it seems we are beyond hope. The outpourings of God have come with power that changes hearts, habits, and hopes, not of just a few people, but even to the very core of a society. The outpourings of God have come in response to prayer. This is the power of prayer.

Epaphras, who is one of you, a bondservant of Christ, greets you, always laboring fervently for you in prayers, that you may stand perfect and complete in all the will of God. For I bear him witness that he has a great zeal for you, and those who are in Laodicea, and those in Hierapolis.

Colossians 4:12-13 (NKJV)

It is time to pray and receive answers from God to meet the needs of people living in the desperate, destructive, and devious times that plague society. Though out history, people have prayed, and God brought His wonderful answers to prayers, even in times and places where it seemed impossible. How about today? Are we, ready and willing to pray for God's wonderful answers? It is time to pray!

Let us pray!

It is time to pray, there is no greater need today than to have Christian men and women of prayer. As Jesus walked here on earth, close to the Father, so we are to walk and pray. Prayer was the key to His success in life and ministry, and it is the key to our success as well. It is time for members of the Body of Christ to rise up and be effective in prayer. The world is desperate for answers; it is waiting and longing for your prayers. It is time to pray!

Article in this book first appeared in the weekly online newsletter *Voice of Thanksgiving.* Over the course of several years, its theme has been and remains that it is time to pray!

Unit One

EMPOWERED FOR PRAYER

My dad was a cabinet maker. He was a craftsman, building wonderful cabinets and furniture. For a few years I worked with my Dad and the bulk of our work was remodeling kitchens and installing cabinets. When people wanted to remodel their kitchen they would call my Dad and over the course of a few weeks, he would walk the home owners through the planning, tear out, and rebuilding phases of the project.

Remodeling is an inexact science, you never know what you might find when you tear out the old cabinets and walls. The rebuilding process could often be taxing. Some jobs went well and then there were the difficult ones. I remember several examples of jobs that were great challenges, with a myriad of unexpected changes, delays, and problems.

To be effective in prayer, we need to do much the same type of things. We must tear out our old and build the new. Old mind sets and patterns of thinking come from the world and worldly thinking. Satan is always ready and willing to supply us with anything we need for doubt, fear, and all the materials for wrong thinking and acting. To follow my remodeling example, all of this must be torn out. The new that replaced it must be based on God's Word or it will be just more of the same old junk. Paul taught that effective prayers require a transformation. We cannot be conformed to this world, but must be transformed by the renewing of our mind. We must be remodeled.

> *I beseech you therefore, brethren, by the mercies of God, that you present your bodies a living sacrifice, holy, acceptable to God, which is your reasonable service. And do not be conformed to this world, but be transformed by the renewing of your mind, that you may prove what is that good and acceptable and perfect will of God.*
>
> ROMANS 12:1-2 (NKJV)

Effective prayer requires a transformation, a renewing of the mind and a new way of thinking. This begins with a new spirit. The person receiving Jesus as Lord becomes a new person and this spiritual rebirth opens the way for the transformation process to begin. In this process the mind is changed little by little until the person thinks, believes, speaks, and acts as the Holy Spirit directs.

For effective prayer there are many areas that must be transformed. For example, we need to understand more of God's nature. He is a good God and He constantly thinks about ways to do us good. He desires that we pray and He is powerful, able, and willing to do great and mighty things, often by answers to our prayers.

When my Dad and I remodeled kitchens we drew up a diagram of the new kitchen and made a list of all the materials and cabinets we would need. For the transformation of our mind we need to have a diagram. Our diagram is based on the Bible. And it shows our transformation to a renewed mind. It is making the changes we need to think, believe, speak, and act like Jesus. He is our diagram, our standard and example.

If then you were raised with Christ, seek those things which are above, where Christ is, sitting at the right hand of God. Set your mind on things above, not on things on the earth. For you died, and your life is hidden with Christ in God.

COLOSSIANS 3:1-3 (NKJV)

Remodeling of our mind is done the same way we originally built up our mind. Growing up we watched how other people walked and copied their actions. We learned to talk and write the same way. Now we need to learn new lessons. We do this by meditating on the Word of God. We can think like Jesus, if we study, meditate on, and practice what the Bible says. The Bible is a guide for living and it provides information on everything needed for right thinking, speaking, and doing.

This Book of the Law shall not depart from your mouth, but you shall meditate in it day and night, that you may observe to do according to all that is written in it. For then you will make your way prosperous, and then you will have good success.

JOSHUA 1:8 (NKJV)

Finally, brethren, whatever things are true, whatever things are noble, whatever things are just, whatever things are pure, whatever things are lovely, whatever things are of good report, if there is any virtue and if there is anything praiseworthy—meditate on these things. The things which you learned and received and heard and saw in me, these do, and the God of peace will be with you.

PHILIPPIANS 4:8-9 (NKJV)

We can apply God's Word to our life and transform our mind. We can put an end to thinking, believing, speaking, and acting like the world and have success in prayer. This takes hard work, but the results will be an effective prayer life that avails much.

Let us pray!

The articles of Unit One—*Empowered for Prayer*, focus on remodeling and how we can be transformed by the Word of God and work of the Holy Spirit to build a Christian life that is empowered for effective prayer.

Article 1

THE FALLOW GROUND

The clock had to be broken; the secondhand seemed to never move. As soon as this last period of the day was over, we would begin Christmas break. Although this was more than 45 years ago, I still can feel the excitement level rising in me and throughout the school. The old building had seen many Christmas breaks, but once again the anticipation built to a higher and higher crescendo. Students were nearly bursting with expectation of the fun and excitement of Christmas break. Finally the last few seconds did pass, the bell rang, and with a hoop and holler, we ran down the hall and out the door.

Life goes tripping along; a day passes on to another day, then weeks, months, and years go by. There are milestones that capture our attention, but mostly, the days just flow one after another. Days are so much like other days; it is hard to even remember anything about them just a week later. What can you say about last Tuesday? Is there something of note about a week ago last Monday? There are days we remember, like the day before Christmas break that I just described, but most days are as James describes life, just a vapor that soon vanishes away.

For what is your life? It is even a vapor that appears for
a little time and then vanishes away.

JAMES 4:14 (NKJV)

However, in contrast to a vapor of our days, most people want their days to count for something. There is an innate part of man, something within the DNA of all men that desires to do something of value. People want to make their life and work count. How about you?

God has called us for this time. And His call is not for just drifting though life, with nothing to show for our time. He has called us to add value to our days and to the days of those around us. This is a high calling in Christ Jesus. Around us we see people, or hear of people, or we read of people, who have taken God at His word and stepped into His call. They do things, accomplish things, they have great fruit. This is what we want for our life.

With this idea in mind, life becomes more like a race, a race we run, to win. There are some fundamentals that will help with our running the race, instead of just watching as our race goes by. First, before we can apply these fundamentals there is a basic requirement: are you a Christian? Have you made Jesus Christ Lord of your life and set your mind and heart to seeking to be His disciple? This is the all important first step for a fruitful life. (For more information on this necessary step, see the section, *Prayer for Salvation*, near the end of this book)

When you are a Christian, you are in a good place for God to work with you and help you. He has made provision for you and your race of life. His provision for a full life begins with your heart. Dealing with the issues of our heart, opens the door for God to work throughout every part of our life. It is His process for building a life of great value and purpose. In Hosea we read of God's plan and process.

Break up your fallow ground, for it is time to seek the
Lord, till He comes and rains righteousness on you.

Hosea 10:12 (NKJV)

The process is straightforward. Step one; break up your fallow ground, this is heart preparation. Step two; seek the Lord, this is effective prayer. Step three; continue until the result comes, the rain of His righteousness. And when God comes and rains righteousness on you, your days will be like those of Jesus; of great value and power.

Breaking up your fallow ground is dealing with the issues of the heart. Please note that this verse from Hosea is not written to the lost; if it was, it would be a command to deal with the land in the wilderness state. Nor is it to backsliders; it does not speak of ground willfully abandoned. This is a command to Christians who have ground that is unproductive due to lack of or limited cultivation. Seed could be sown and rain given, but the yield would be meager at best, because the ground is not prepared. Isn't this the state we find in much of the church today? Isn't this the state of the heart of many people; vast tracts of fallow ground. Is this the state of your heart?

The fallow ground of the unprepared heart is first of all hard. It is insensitive to sin and unresponsive to the still small voice of the Holy Spirit. Hardness of heart leads to the life of the Pharisee. The hard heart is formal and cold. It fulfills religious duty, but with little fruit of holiness or effective ministry, and is characterized by a lack of God's power.

having a form of godliness but denying its power. And
from such people turn away!

always learning and never able to come to the knowledge
of the truth.

2 Timothy 3:5 and 7 (NKJV)

7

"Today, if you will hear His voice, do not harden your hearts as in the rebellion."

HEBREWS 3:15 (NKJV)

The fallow ground of the unprepared heart is also weed covered ground. Jeremiah also writes about fallow ground. His admonition is also to break up the fallow ground, and then he goes on to instruct us, not to sow among thorns. The world and its ways are the weeds and thorns in many hearts. These weeds must be dealt with if we are going to have fruitful harvests and value of abundance in our life.

The problem of weeds is currently an epidemic. Never in history have weed seeds been more available. At the same time there is less teaching and training, on how to deal with weeds. If we allow weeds to flourish, it leaves our hearts unsuitable for effective cultivation. "As the gardener well knows, the weeds need not be willfully encouraged in order to flourish; they are the product of sloth, indifference, and neglect", writes Arthur Wallis in his book on praying for revival, *In the Day of Thy Power*:

> *For thus says the Lord to the men of Judah and Jerusalem: "Break up your fallow ground, and do not sow among thorns. Circumcise yourselves to the Lord, and take away the foreskins of your hearts, You men of Judah and inhabitants of Jerusalem, lest My fury come forth like fire, and burn so that no one can quench it, because of the evil of your doings."*
>
> JEREMIAH 4:3-4 (NKJV)

> *I went by the field of the lazy man, and by the vineyard of the man devoid of understanding; and there it was, all overgrown with thorns; its surface was covered with nettles; its stone wall was broken down.*
>
> PROVERBS 24:30-31 (NKJV)

And some fell among thorns, and the thorns sprang up and choked them.

Now he who received seed among the thorns is he who hears the word, and the cares of this world and the deceitfulness of riches choke the word, and he becomes unfruitful.

MATTHEW 13:7 AND 22 (NKJV)

The fallow ground of the unprepared heart is unproductive and unprofitable. Hard and weed infested ground will not yield a good harvest, even if God poured out His blessing, there would be no great harvest, the ground would remain unfruitful.

This is not what God wants, He expects us to be fruitful. God commanded Adam to tend the garden and be fruitful. When Noah left the ark this same command came once again, be fruitful. Jesus declared the fields were white; that is ready for harvest. He told us to pray for laborers for the harvest; this is being fruitful and it is what He expects of you and me.

For the earth which drinks in the rain that often comes upon it, and bears herbs useful for those by whom it is cultivated, receives blessing from God; but if it bears thorns and briars, it is rejected and near to being cursed, whose end is to be burned.

HEBREWS 6:7-8 (NKJV)

Every branch in Me that does not bear fruit He takes away; and every branch that bears fruit He prunes, that it may bear more fruit.

JOHN 15:2 (NKJV)

9

I am the vine, you are the branches. He who abides in Me, and I in him, bears much fruit; for without Me you can do nothing.

JOHN 15:5 (NKJV)

But also for this very reason, giving all diligence, add to your faith virtue, to virtue knowledge, to knowledge self-control, to self-control perseverance, to perseverance godliness, to godliness brotherly kindness, and to brotherly kindness love. For if these things are yours and abound, you will be neither barren nor unfruitful in the knowledge of our Lord Jesus Christ.

2 PETER 1:5-8 (NKJV)

This is a good time to allow the Holy Spirit to reveal the condition of your heart and show you any place of hardness or weeds. Ask Him to reveal to you the true nature of your heart and how to deal with what He reveals to you. To be effective in prayer we need to break up the fallow ground.

Let us pray!

Article 2

REVELATIONS

A look through the catalog revealed all kinds of items, from toys to appliances. And you did not need money; all you had to do was to take the books to the store and redeem them for the item you wanted. The books where filled with S & H Green Stamps.

This was a popular form of trading stamps used in the United States from 1930s until the 1980s. The stamps were distributed by supermarkets, gas filling stations, and many stores. They were given as a bonus to shoppers, much as some credit cards give awards (such as mileage or cash back) for shopping. Each book when filled was worth 1200 points and could be redeemed in special Green Stamp stores. It was fun to get the stamps and fill the books. It was great to go with my Mom to the store and get items for "free".

One of the great missionaries of the nineteenth century was Hudson Taylor. Until the mid 1800s, all of the empire of China was closed to the Gospel, except for small pockets around the port cities like Canton. Taylor changed all of that. Think about what he did, he was able to go to China, minister to thousands of people all over China, start the China Inland Mission, and open many mission works in the inland provinces of China. These are great accomplishments for a man who started with and often had no support or backing. And yet there is more to the story and this is the key for us today. Hudson Taylor said, "When God decided to evangelize inland China, He looked around to find a man who was weak enough for Him to use".

> *Finally, my brethren, be strong in the Lord and in the*
> *power of His might.*
>
> EPHESIANS 6:10 (NKJV)

This is what God wants with us; for us to be weak enough for Him to use. We have gone to great lengths to do what we think we can do and tried to do it in our strength and abilities, by our ways and plans. However, now it is time to begin to do the seemingly impossible, and God works with and through men and women of prayer, weak enough for His power and glory to be their strength.

To help us make this transition from personal weakness to His strength manifest in our life, we must be established in Him and in His gift of salvation. There are seven revelations that make men and women weak enough for Christ to use and make strong in prayer. When we have made these revelations a reality in our life, receiving and meditating on them, until they are real in our heart and mind, then we will walk and pray with power in our new life, and will have exchanged our weakness for His empowerment.

> *He will not be afraid of evil tidings; his heart is steadfast,*
> *trusting in the Lord. His heart is established; he will*
> *not be afraid, until he sees his desire upon his enemies.*
>
> PSALM 112:7-8 (NKJV)

To help us remember these revelations, I have included, for each one, a short quip or story. The first four are in this article and the next three in the following article.

REALITY OF REDEMPTION

Redemption means to buy up or ransom. This is what Christ did for us; He redeemed us from the curse. A way for us to remember this is the Green Stamp program. Mom and I would take the books of stamps and redeem them for great household items.

Christ, by His death and resurrection, has redeemed us from the curse of the law. He paid the price of the curse due to us, so we could live under the blessing of Abraham. There is a great description of the blessing and curse in chapter 28 of the book of Deuteronomy. The first 15 verses present the blessing and by redemption we have this blessing.

> *Christ has redeemed us from the curse of the law, having become a curse for us (for it is written, "Cursed is everyone who hangs on a tree"), that the blessing of Abraham might come upon the Gentiles in Christ Jesus, that we might receive the promise of the Spirit through faith.*
>
> GALATIANS 3:13-14 (NKJV)

Redemption has been obtained for us by Christ; it is a done deal, completed 2000 years ago on the cross. Our redemption is an eternal redemption, the victory was over Satan and all his forces and it was, and is, a full and complete victory that lasts forever. And our redemption is not just something we get later in Heaven, it is operational now and is ours. If you are in Christ, then redemption is a reality. You are no longer under the curse, no longer under the dominance of Satan. You have great authority as a redeemed believer in Christ. Redeemed!

> *But Christ came as High Priest of the good things to come, with the greater and more perfect tabernacle not made with hands, that is, not of this creation. Not with the blood of goats and calves, but with His own blood He entered the Most Holy Place once for all, having*

obtained eternal redemption. For if the blood of bulls and goats and the ashes of a heifer, sprinkling the unclean, sanctifies for the purifying of the flesh, how much more shall the blood of Christ, who through the eternal Spirit offered Himself without spot to God, cleanse your conscience from dead works to serve the living God?

HEBREWS 9:11-14 (NKJV)

REALITY OF THE NEW BIRTH

When I was young there was a show on TV that was very popular, the show was so popular that it has continued in various forms, off and on, until today; the show, "To Tell the Truth". In this show three people claim to be a person and the panel of stars must determine, by asking questions, which ones are imposters. At the end of the show the announcer says something like, "Will the real David Williamson, please stand up!" And the one who is not an imposter, the real person, stands up.

The second reality is that of the new birth. By new birth, we are a new creation in Christ; once we are born again, we are the new person, the real person we are designed to be. The person I was before I was born again is dead. The old things, nature, and ways of thing and acting are gone.

When at the end of the show the announcer says, "Will the real David Williamson, please stand up" this is what should happen in our life; the new man standing up and living as the born again, new creation in Christ. This new man is reconciled to God and empowered by God for action (including effective, fervent prayers that avail much!). A new creation in Christ!

Therefore, if anyone is in Christ, he is a new creation; old things have passed away; behold, all things have become new. Now all things are of God, who has reconciled us to Himself through Jesus Christ, and has given us the ministry of reconciliation,

2 Corinthians 5:17-18 (NKJV)

by which have been given to us exceedingly great and precious promises, that through these you may be partakers of the divine nature, having escaped the corruption that is in the world through lust.

2 Peter 1:4 (NKJV)

For we are His workmanship, created in Christ Jesus for good works, which God prepared beforehand that we should walk in them.

Ephesians 2:10 (NKJV)

REALITY OF BEING MADE THE RIGHTEOUSNESS OF GOD

Coming home from a trip to a conference in Costa Rica, I was stopped at customs in Miami. They took me to a special room and made me sit and wait, and wait, and wait. I could see the customs official working feverishly on a computer and then he was joined by another official. The first man kept pointing to me and then pointing to the computer. Finally, they came to me and said I could go. I said thank you, but I was curious. "What was this about?" They said they were looking for a man named David Williamson, but by looking at my passport they became convinced it was a different David Williamson. So I was free to go and enter the US. Thank God for my passport.

Being made the righteousness of God is having right standing with God. Christ took my sin so that I might have His righteousness. When I stand before the Father, I do so with Jesus' righteousness. This is a wonderful place to be; in right standing with God! This is like having a passport for the country of Heaven that says I have permission and authority to live in Heaven and enjoy all of the benefits of citizenship. This is a wonderful position, the righteousness of God!

> *For He made Him who knew no sin to be sin for us, that we might become the righteousness of God in Him.*
>
> 2 CORINTHIANS 5:21 (NKJV)

> *But now the righteousness of God apart from the law is revealed, being witnessed by the Law and the Prophets, even the righteousness of God, through faith in Jesus Christ, to all and on all who believe. For there is no difference; for all have sinned and fall short of the glory of God, being justified freely by His grace through the redemption that is in Christ Jesus, whom God set forth as a propitiation by His blood, through faith, to demonstrate His righteousness, because in His forbearance God had passed over the sins that were previously committed, to demonstrate at the present time His righteousness, that He might be just and the justifier of the one who has faith in Jesus. Where is boasting then? It is excluded. By what law? Of works? No, but by the law of faith.*
>
> ROMANS 3:21-27 (NKJV)

This position is an important key to effective prayer. Please note the benefits given to those people who have right standing (righteousness) with God. This includes the promise of God hearing their prayers and the promise of prayers that avail much!

> *For the eyes of the Lord are on the righteous, and His ears are open to their prayers; but the face of the Lord is against those who do evil.*
>
> 1 PETER 3:12 (NKJV)

Confess your trespasses to one another, and pray for one another, that you may be healed. The effective, fervent prayer of a righteous man avails much.

JAMES 5:16 (NKJV)

REALITY OF BEING GOD-INDWELT

One of the very popular stories, found in comics, books, radio, and television, is that of Superman. For decades Clark Kent, mild mannered reporter for the Daily Planet newspaper, would, when calamity struck, become Superman and fight for truth, justice, and the American way. While Superman is just a character from the comics, being God-indwelt is like being a super hero.

Christians seem like other people on the outside, but on the inside there is the Superhero of all heroes, God Himself. The reality of the Christian life is that we live with God for us, God with us, and God in us. The result of this is far greater power than even superman could claim. The creator of the universe lives inside each Christian.

Fear not, for I am with you; be not dismayed, for I am your God. I will strengthen you, yes, I will help you, I will uphold you with My righteous right hand.

ISAIAH 41:10 (NKJV)

And what agreement has the temple of God with idols? For you are the temple of the living God. As God has said: "I will dwell in them and walk among them. I will be their God, and they shall be My people."

2 CORINTHIANS 6:16 (NKJV)

The reality of God-indwelt is walking with God, and it is so much more. He is in us, walking with us and His power is powerful in us. When we walk, He walks and when we lay hands on someone for healing, God lays His hand on the person. When we pray, He prays with us! The Greater One dwells within us, God-indwelt!

This is the first four of our realities; redemption, new birth, righteous, and God-indwelt. We need to establish these in our heart and mind. As we meditate and act on these revelations, we exchange our weakness for His great and mighty strength. In the next article we will continue and look further at how to establish these revelations in our life.

Let us pray!

Article 3

MORE REVELATIONS

W hen I was station on an Air Force base in Germany, I worked as an umpire for Little League Baseball. There were many teams in the area; this provided a lot of fun for many boys. Unfortunately, as sometimes happens, there were some problems between the parents and the umpires. Most of the umpires were young GIs, but many of the parents were senior NCOs and officers. It was very difficult for the young, low ranking, umpires to control the game and the fans.

The problem got so bad one summer that the Base Commander had to step in. He sent out a memo explaining from the time the game began, until it was finished, the umpire had the same authority as the Base Commander. Suddenly, when an umpire told parents to get back in the stands or to stop shouting things at players, they listened and followed what he said to do.

In the previous article we began a study of the realities of the great exchange of personal weakness for the strength of the Lord. We mentioned the great missionary Hudson Taylor and his quote about his call to evangelize in China. He said, "When God decided to evangelize inland China, He looked around to find a man who was weak enough for Him to use". This is what God wants with us; for us to be weak enough for Him to be strong in us.

Finally, my brethren, be strong in the Lord and in the power of His might.

 EPHESIANS 6:10 (NKJV)

To help us make this transition from personal weakness to His strength manifest in our life, we must be established in Him and in His gift of salvation. There are seven revelations that make weak enough to be used, men and women, strong in Christ. In the last article we saw the first four revelations and now we will continue our list. Our goal is to establish these great truths in our heart, life, and prayers.

REALITY OF REDEMPTION

Green Stamps—I am redeemed by Christ

REALITY OF THE NEW BIRTH

To Tell the Truth—New birth makes me a new me

REALITY OF BEING MADE THE RIGHTEOUSNESS OF GOD

The Passport—I am the righteousness of God

REALITY OF BEING GOD-INDWELT
The Super Hero—God indwelt, the ultimate Super Hero

And now realities number five through seven.

REALITY OF THE AUTHORITY IN THE NAME OF JESUS
When the Base Commander sent out that memo, he was giving the umpires the authority of his name. The strength they received from the memo was not because he was physically strong, but there was power

in the name of the position; the Base Commander. For example, a man could be sent home to the states, just by having orders written above the Base Commander's name.

Jesus has a name far above that of the Base Commander or even the Commander in Chief (the President of the United States). The name of Jesus is the name above all names. Every power and authority is subject to His name. God has given Jesus the name that is over everything in heaven, on earth, and under the earth. The name of Jesus is the greatest authority and power anywhere!

The Base Commander gave the umpires the use of his name, giving them his authority and power for the time of the game. Jesus has given Christians the use of His name. This is the giving of unlimited power and this power is backed by the authority of this great name. It is like, but so much better, having unlimited use of Bill Gates' credit card. We have the authority of the name of Jesus!

Therefore God also has highly exalted Him and given Him the name which is above every name, that at the name of Jesus every knee should bow, of those in heaven, and of those on earth, and of those under the earth, and that every tongue should confess that Jesus Christ is Lord, to the glory of God the Father.

PHILIPPIANS 2:9-11 (NKJV)

God, who at various times and in various ways spoke in time past to the fathers by the prophets, has in these last days spoken to us by His Son, whom He has appointed heir of all things, through whom also He made the worlds; who being the brightness of His glory and the express image of His person, and upholding all things by the word of His power, when He had by Himself purged our sins, sat down at the right hand of the Majesty on high, having become so much better than the angels, as He has by inheritance obtained a more excellent name than they.

Hebrews 1:1-4 (NKJV)

And in that day you will ask Me nothing. Most assuredly, I say to you, whatever you ask the Father in My name He will give you.

John 16:23 (NKJV)

REALITY OF THE INTEGRITY OF GOD'S WORD

Many years ago, my wife and I decided to buy the house we were renting. We talked to a lending agency and did the preparation work and then signed about a million pieces of paper. The documents spelled out the requirements, for both sides, of the agreement. When we were finished, we knew that as long as we did our part (a bunch of house payments) the house was ours.

There was a time when all a man needed was a handshake. The handshake was their commitment to do what they said they would do. Mighty corporations were bought and sold, with nothing more than a handshake. From the handshake we came to the contract, this was a written form that spelled out the details of an agreement. The handshake or contract was the bond of commitment to do what the contract said, based on the integrity of the parties involved. Integrity is an unimpaired condition, a firm adherence, and being complete and undivided. Simply, put, it is doing what you say you will do.

God has said He is committed to His Word; He will do what is written in His Word. His handshake with us, His contract with us; is that He will do what He has promised. We can trust the Word, even with our life, because of God's integrity. He is unimpaired by any condition that would make Him change or go back on His Word. He is firm in His adherence to the promises of the Word. And He is completely committed and undivided in His assurance that His word is true; He will act on it as He promised. This is the covenant between God and man, God's Word is established and true; He will do what He has said!

So shall My word be that goes forth from My mouth; it shall not return to Me void, but it shall accomplish what I please, and it shall prosper in the thing for which I sent it.
ISAIAH 55:11 (NKJV)

And they went out and preached everywhere, the Lord working with them and confirming the word through the accompanying signs. Amen.
MARK 16:20 (NKJV)

REALITY OF THE GOD KIND OF FAITH RESIDING IN YOU

Archie Manning was a great football quarterback; he was one of the best. While attending the University of Mississippi he set many records for passing. Although the team was not very good, people recognized Archie as great. He was drafted by the National Football League to play for the New Orleans Saints team. Once again the team he played on was not very good, but Archie was great. He was player of the year several years and played in the Pro-Bowl, the game for players deemed the best at their position.

Maybe his greatest accomplishment was having three sons, Cooper, Peyton, and Eli. All three received Archie's football quarterback genes, Cooper was a great football player, but had a short career due to a spinal disease. Peyton and Eli have both won the Super Bowl, the championship for football!

Everything we do in the Christian life is by faith and we have received faith from our Father, His kind of faith. In Mark 11 Jesus said, "Have faith in God". This has been translated as "Have the God kind of faith." And this is what we have. We have been made partakers of God's divine nature and His divine nature includes faith. God gives faith and this gift is given to each man (that includes you!). Faith comes from the Word of God and it overcomes the world with a great victory!

> *For by grace you have been saved through faith, and that not of yourselves; it is the gift of God, not of works, lest anyone should boast.*
>
> EPHESIANS 2:8-9 (NKJV)

> *So then faith comes by hearing, and hearing by the word of God.*
>
> ROMANS 10:17 (NKJV)

> *For I say, through the grace given to me, to everyone who is among you, not to think of himself more highly than he ought to think, but to think soberly, as God has dealt to each one a measure of faith.*
>
> ROMANS 12:3 (NKJV)

> *Whoever believes that Jesus is the Christ is born of God, and everyone who loves Him who begot also loves him who is begotten of Him.*
>
> 1 JOHN 5:1 (NKJV)

> *For whatever is born of God overcomes the world. And this is the victory that has overcome the world—our faith.*
>
> 1 JOHN 5:4 (NKJV)

AND DO

There you have them, seven revelations and you have a way to remember them. However, to make them a reality in your life you need to do three things. First, you need to meditate on these realities, focusing on the Bible verses. This is how you transfer these from just head knowledge to heart knowledge. Second, you need to begin to declare these realities in your life. Regardless of what you see or feel, saying what God says about these realities makes them real in your life. And third, do them. Faith is an action word and is effective in the life of those who act on their faith.

This Book of the Law shall not depart from your mouth, but you shall meditate in it day and night, that you may observe to do according to all that is written in it. For then you will make your way prosperous, and then you will have good success.

JOSHUA 1:8 (NKJV)

But his delight is in the law of the Lord, and in His law he meditates day and night. His heart is fixed and established

PSALM 1:2 (NKJV)

But do you want to know, O foolish man, that faith without works is dead? Was not Abraham our father justified by works when he offered Isaac his son on the altar? Do you see that faith was working together with his works, and by works faith was made perfect?

JAMES 2:20-22 (NKJV)

When we are established in these realities, we will make the transition from personal weakness to Christ's strength, and His strength will be manifest in our life and prayers. These seven revelations can take us from being weak to strong in Christ, empowered to pray!

Let us pray!

THE STUMBLE

W hen my friend Mark and I were in the ninth grade, we went with Mark's Dad to Fort Morgan, Colorado, to see our home town high school football team play against the team from Fort Morgan. It was a terrific battle, both teams fighting hard, but nether team was able to move the ball very far. Fort Morgan had kicked a field goal and lead, 3 to 0, late in the final period. With only a few minutes left in the game, the Longmont running back, Rich van Felt, broke through the line and out of a near tackle and ran more than forty yards for what was the winning score. And although Mark and I were shivering with the cold of the night, we were warmed by the thrill of victory.

Twenty years later I was asked to help coach a local high school football team. One afternoon the head coach and I were making plans for the next practice and began to talk about games we had seen. I told the story of going to Fort Morgan. And while Pat (the head coach) listened closely, soon after I began the story, he got this pained look on his face. When I finished he explained, "I played in that game." "I remember the play you described. I was the guy who made that last attempted tackle. "I had stumbled trying to make the tackle and could not get a good grip on von Felt. He broke free, made that long run, and scored. Von Felt had shoes with a red sole, and as I lay on the ground, after he broke the tackle, I watched those red soles go down the field, knowing our chance of making the playoffs had come to an end."

In Matthew (Matthew 11:6), Jesus tells us, *"And blessed is he who is not offended because of Me."* The word is translated, "offended", in both the King James and New King James Versions and is translated as "stumbling" in the New American Standard Version. The word in the Greek is *skandalizo*; (scandalize) it means to entrap, trip, or entice. In this verse Jesus is presenting an important key to successful Christian living and for effective prayer. We are not to stumble over Him.

At first glance this seems very strange. Stumble over Jesus, you must be kidding, He is Lord, He is my Lord. However, the fact of the matter is that many people, including many Christians, do stumble over Jesus. This stumbling began before Jesus was even born. Men stumbled over prophesies of Jesus' appearing. And there has been stumbling ever since. How we deal with stumbling is of great importance to our success.

Salvation revolves around Jesus and our response to Him. If we receive Him as Lord, we receive new life. If we reject Him as Lord, we remain in the hold of sin and death. For centuries men have stumbled over this choice and unfortunately, many have rejected Him. Some try to make things harder, by adding additional ways and means that one must follow to have new life. Others have claimed requirements of belonging to a specific group or organization. Still others have tried to throw out the entire question, claiming no standard or requirement at all. However, the Bible is very clear that there is one way to God and all who come to God must come through belief in Christ Jesus. This is the only way to salvation. To attempt by any other means, is to stumble over Jesus.

> *Then Jesus said to them again, "Most assuredly, I say to you, I am the door of the sheep. All who ever came before Me are thieves and robbers, but the sheep did not hear them. I am the door. If anyone enters by Me, he will be saved, and will go in and out and find pasture. The thief*

does not come except to steal, and to kill, and to destroy.
I have come that they may have life, and that they may
have it more abundantly. I am the good shepherd. The
good shepherd gives His life for the sheep".

JOHN 10:7-11 (NKJV)

Beyond dealing with this most important stumbling block, there remain other opportunities to stumble. Jesus states there are great blessings for believers who do not stumble. This has vital importance to our life and our prayers. We need to recognize places where we stumble and deal with them. It would be good for us to review common points of stumbling. The Greek word for stumbling is useful for this purpose; remember it means to entice, to trip, and to entrap.

The Devil often uses enticement to cause people to stumble. He likes to use this to keep people from salvation and to draw them further into sin. His goal is to draw them in so deep, they believe there is no way out and no hope. The Devil also uses enticement against Christians. He hates God and so he works to destroy everything that reminds him of God, including Christians. His enticement is individualized for each person; he looks for areas of weakness, fear, doubt, or unbelief. He then entices the person with something in that area.

Men and women, who seek Jesus and the fullness of the life He has prepared for us, can have abundant life. However, the abundant life comes only in Christ Jesus. Stumbling often comes through trying to live a combination life, combining living in Christ with living in the world. If we are seeking things without Christ, anything outside of Christ, then we are a candidate for enticing and stumbling.

Yet indeed I also count all things loss for the excellence of
the knowledge of Christ Jesus my Lord, for whom I have
suffered the loss of all things, and count them as rubbish,
that I may gain Christ and be found in Him, not having

my own righteousness, which is from the law, but that
which is through faith in Christ, the righteousness which
is from God by faith; that I may know Him and the power
of His resurrection, and the fellowship of His sufferings,
being conformed to His death, if, by any means, I may
attain to the resurrection from the dead.

PHILIPPIANS 3:8-11 (NKJV)

Another common means of stumbling is by tripping. For example, people trip over sin and can make this into a point of stumbling over Jesus, if they do not receive His forgiveness. (Forgiveness must be done His way), and this can be a stumbling block as well.

If we say that we have no sin, we deceive ourselves,
and the truth is not in us. If we confess our sins, He is
faithful and just to forgive us our sins and to cleanse
us from all unrighteousness. If we say that we have not
sinned, we make Him a liar, and His word is not in us.

1 JOHN 1:8-10 (NKJV)

Beyond the tripping on sin, there are other problems; there are other things that people can trip over. A very common example of this is to trip due to our traditions. The Pharisees missed the Messiah. They tripped over Jesus, because He did not fit their traditions.

Traditions are very common and some can be very good, but some can cause stumbling. There is an old saying, "The cross is where my will and God's will cross." If I am to live a successful Christian life and be effective in prayer, then my will must change to His will in all things. The same can be said of traditions, everywhere my tradition, crosses His tradition, my tradition must change.

We also can be tripped up by making excuses. A common area of excuses involves limiting the power of God. People also make excuses to allow worldliness in their life. There are excuses made to accept all kinds of assumptions, rumors, and lies, over the Word of God.

The word, entrap, means to catch in a trap or to lure into danger, error, difficulty, a compromising situation, or embarrassment This is a stumbling block that is common and also can be very subtle. The Devil likes to work a person into a bad situation that could ruin a reputation, a testimony, or causes the person to be ineffective or cause them to quit.

A great example of this is the compromising situation, that is a place or action that is not sin, but has the appearance of evil. There are things that may be okay for others, but if we are going to walk in the fullness of the Christian life God has prepared for us and if we are going to be effective in prayer, we must not have even the appearance of evil.

> *All things are lawful for me, but all things are not helpful. All things are lawful for me, but I will not be brought under the power of any.*
> 1 Corinthians 6:12 (NKJV)

My friend Pat (head coach of the team, who stumbled instead of making the tackle in the football game years ago) claims that if he had taken one more step over to his right, he could have hit the runner square on and made the tackle. He is sure if he had made that tackle, they would have won and made the playoffs. All he needed was one more step.

For Christians we are called to make one more step to keep from stumbling. If we take the step to depart from iniquity we can keep from stumbling. Paul describes this as being a vessel for honor, useful for the Master. As men and women of prayer this is what we want, to be useful bringing God's power and His answers to this world, by prayer.

> *Nevertheless the solid foundation of God stands, having this seal: "The Lord knows those who are His," and, "Let everyone who names the name of Christ depart*

from iniquity." But in a great house there are not only vessels of gold and silver, but also of wood and clay, some for honor and some for dishonor. Therefore if anyone cleanses himself from the latter, he will be a vessel for honor, sanctified and useful for the Master, prepared for every good work. Flee also youthful lusts; but pursue righteousness, faith, love, peace with those who call on the Lord out of a pure heart. But avoid foolish and ignorant disputes, knowing that they generate strife. And a servant of the Lord must not quarrel but be gentle to all, able to teach, patient, in humility correcting those who are in opposition, if God perhaps will grant them repentance, so that they may know the truth, and that they may come to their senses and escape the snare of the devil, having been taken captive by him to do his will.

2 TIMOTHY 2:19-26 (NKJV)

Our salvation in Christ provides remedy for all the forms of stumbling. The key is for us to take the steps prescribed, for example, to be cleansed. This comes by drawing close to Jesus in a daily relationship, and then fleeing from and avoiding those things that take us away from Him. This includes being careful to not give even the appearance of evil.

It is very important that we walk with Christ and not stumble. He is looking for men and women in whom He can show Himself strong. Men and women who will not stumble, who cannot be enticed, tripped, or entrapped.

But know this, that in the last days perilous times will come: For men will be lovers of themselves, lovers of money, boasters, proud, blasphemers, disobedient to parents, unthankful, unholy, unloving, unforgiving, slanderers, without self-control, brutal, despisers of good, traitors, headstrong, haughty, lovers of pleasure rather than lovers of God, having a form of godliness but denying its power. And from such people turn away!

2 TIMOTHY 3:1-5 (NKJV)

Let us pray!

Article 5

WHO DO YOU SAY I AM?

T he Bible is filled with amazing events, one that has always caught
my attention is found in the fifth chapter of the book of Daniel.
King Belshazzar was having a banquet, and he was wallowing in the
debauchery of his rule and reign as king. He and his quests were filled
with pride. The lessons from his father's life, recorded earlier in this book
of the Bible, meant nothing to Belshazzar.

Suddenly a hand appeared and began writing on the wall of the
palace; everyone at the banquet was scared. No one was able to interpret
the meaning of the writing, so in desperation they called for help. Daniel
came and explained the meaning of the words.

And this is the inscription that was written:

MENE, MENE, TEKEL, UPHARSIN.
This is the interpretation of each word. Mene: God has
numbered your kingdom, and finished it; Tekel: You
have been weighed in the balances, and found wanting;
Peres: Your kingdom has been divided, and given to the
Medes and Persians.

DANIEL 5:25-28 (NKJV)

What a powerful statement; *"You have been weighed in the balances"*. It was catastrophic for this king, but everyone faces times of being weighed. And one day each of us will stand before Jesus and give an account of our life; this is the ultimate weighing or judgment. For those who have given their life to Jesus, this will be a judgment of their works. For those persons who have never made Jesus Lord of their life, it will be the day of final judgment.

"You have been weighed in the balances" This statement should also be applied on a regular basis as an examination of our life, works, and prayers. Daily, the Word of God and Holy Spirit, weighs us; they measure what and how we are doing. They do this as part of their ongoing guidance of our daily walk; working to bring a transformation to how we live. They are like a mirror, revealing to us areas where we need to grow and mature. The goal is to show us the areas that are not like our great example, Jesus. These areas are shown to us, to guide us in making the changes we needed; so we will walk and pray in faith, and be, in everyway, more like Jesus.

> *But we all, with unveiled face, beholding as in a mirror the glory of the Lord, are being transformed into the same image from glory to glory, just as by the Spirit of the Lord.*
>
> 2 CORINTHIANS 3:18 (NKJV)

> *by which have been given to us exceedingly great and precious promises, that through these you may be partakers of the divine nature, having escaped the corruption that is in the world through lust.*
>
> 2 PETER 1:4 (NKJV)

This weighing or evaluation process is very important, especially for effective prayer. If we are going to be powerful in prayer, we will be weighed in the balance, by the Word and the Holy Spirit. They will look at every area of our life, including our words, deeds, character, relationships, and faith. We are a new creation in Christ, we have the mind of Christ, we can do all things through Christ who gives us strength, and Jesus is the author and finisher of our faith, so when we are weighed, we should not be lacking in the things we need for effective prayer.

> *and be found in Him, not having my own righteousness,*
> *which is from the law, but that which is through faith in*
> *Christ, the righteousness which is from God by faith;*
> PHILIPPIANS 3:9 (NKJV)

One of the most important areas of weighing for effective prayers is looking at one aspect of how we pray. Do we pray in faith or in the flesh? This battle has raged in people since the time of Adam and Eve in the Garden. The flesh tries to rule and dominate everything we do. The flesh also tries to dominate our prayers. Even when we are walking in faith, the flesh often gets in the way, hindering our prayer, causing us to stumble, or clouding the issues; anything to keep us from effective prayer.

There is a battle that rages between the new creation and the "old man". It is easy to slip back into the old ways and this is why we need consistent examination. Peter is a good example of having to deal with this battle. He shows us how quick and easy it is, to cross over from faith to flesh.

In the book of Matthew, in the course of just a few verses, Peter moves from a faith statement to a flesh statement. When asked by Jesus, *"Who do you say I am?" "You are the Christ, the Son of the living God"* was Peter's answer. This was not a statement from his natural knowledge; it was a revelation from the Father, given by the Holy Spirit, a faith statement. However, moments later, when Jesus taught that He would have to go to Jerusalem and suffer, be killed, and raised on the third day,

Peter said, *". . . this shall not happen to You!"* This was a statement from the desires of his flesh.

We all have had opportunities to speak in faith or to speak in our flesh. And this can carry over into our prayers. Efforts to be effective in prayer must deal with hindrances. They are lurking around, waiting to trip us up. Also praying comes with its own built in problems, after all problems are what we are praying about. It is easy to slip and get caught-up in the problem, and try to pray what we feel, instead of by faith. In the moment of battle, what comes out of your mouth, prayers of faith or flesh?

Since, in Christ, we have the victory, why do we sometime fail? There are things in us, beliefs, attitudes, practices, and sins that must be exposed by the light of the Word and the work of the Holy Spirit. The Bible, especially the New Testament, is a guidebook, teaching success in the faith verses flesh battle. It records that there are many things we can do to have success and that ultimate success is to be like Jesus.

There are several keys to building success in the faith verses flesh battle. Here are two of those keys. The first is having an abundance of the Word in our heart, for out of the abundance of the heart the mouth speaks. If your heart has only a little Word in it, then some of the time you may speak and pray in faith. But, this sets you up to be like Peter in our example, he spoke in faith and then moments later he spoke in the flesh.

When the pressure is on, you want to have your heart full to overflowing with the Word of God, so you will pray in faith, praying effectual fervent prayers that avail much. To do this you need to daily fill your heart, to the point of overflowing, with more and more of the Word of God.

A second key to build success in this battle is the careful guarding of your heart. We live in difficult times, and while this is one of the reasons it is so important for us to pray, it is also a cause of great obstacles to effective prayer. Worldly desires work to damage your heart and insure the flesh coming out, in both the words we speak and our prayers.

Now the works of the flesh are evident, which are: adultery, fornication, uncleanness, lewdness, idolatry, sorcery, hatred, contentions, jealousies, outbursts of wrath, selfish ambitions, dissensions, heresies, envy, murders, drunkenness, revelries, and the like; of which I tell you beforehand, just as I also told you in time past, that those who practice such things will not inherit the kingdom of God.

GALATIANS 5:19-21 (NKJV)

Every day, all through the day, these works, in various forms, are bombarding us. They come in our newspapers, on the radio and TV, in movies and videos, in conversations, and phone calls. If we are not careful they will blast holes in our heart and attempt to stop us from praying or make our prayers, prayers of flesh instead of prayers of faith. The man or woman of effective prayer will guard their heart, diligently.

My son, give attention to my words; Incline your ear to my sayings. Do not let them depart from your eyes; Keep them in the midst of your heart; For they are life to those who find them, And health to all their flesh. Keep your heart with all diligence, For out of it spring the issues of life.

PROVERBS 4:20-23 (NKJV)

A good man out of the good treasure of his heart brings forth good; and an evil man out of the evil treasure of his heart brings forth evil. For out of the abundance of the heart his mouth speaks.

LUKE 6:45 (NKJV)

We can be successful in prayer. Our success comes by praying in faith and not in the flesh. Filling our heart with the Word of God and diligently guarding our heart are two keys to success. What is the Holy Spirit saying to you? Are you ready for battle? Are you ready for success?

"You have been weighed in the balances"

Let us pray!

Article 6

LIGHT

I was driving a van with a team of people in Croatia several years ago. We were going through a mountainous area, where most of the roads were narrow and winding. There were sharp turns, steep climbs, and we passed through several tunnels. One time we entered a long dark tunnel. We had been in bright sunlight before we drove into the darkness of the tunnel and this, coupled with the lack of lights and reflectors on the walls, made this tunnel seem very dark.

Just before we entered the tunnel, a guy went around me on a motorcycle. This was a long tunnel and it was so dark in the tunnel that quickly I began to watch intently the taillight of this motorcycle as a guide a little beyond the light of my headlights. I followed for some time and then suddenly the taillight from the motorcycle disappeared.

One moment it was there and then it was gone. I thought he must have fallen and so I began to slow down and get ready to stop. Just as I got the van slowed down, my headlights picked out a turn in the tunnel. This was not a curve, but a 90°right turn. The motorcyclist had not fallen, he had turned the corner! By slowing down because of the taillight disappearing, I was able to safely make the turn. Thank God for the light. I have speculated that the Lord sent the motorcycle to help me and have wondered what would have happened if I had not been slowed by the question of what happened to the light.

Let me ask you a question, what do we know about God and His nature? The common answer of course is God is love. 1 John 4:8 and 16 and other verses tell us this answer and this answer is correct. So then just when we have that settled, we read 1 John1:5.

> *This is the message which we have heard from Him and declare to you, that God is light and in Him is no darkness at all.*
>
> 1 JOHN 1:5 (NKJV)

If we read with our knowledge, instead our eyes, we read it like this; *this is the message which we have heard from Him and declare to you, that God is love and in Him is no darkness at all.* However, that is not what is says! Read it again. And this time read it carefully.

> *This is the message which we have heard from Him and declare to you, that God is light and in Him is no darkness at all.*
>
> 1 JOHN 1:5 (NKJV)

We all know that God is love, but John clearly explains to us that God is also light. This is very important to see this and understand the importance of this duel nature of God, He is love and He is also light. The two are different and some understanding of both is vital to a successful Christian life and effective prayer.

When dealing with sin, we must know both the love and light of God. If we understand and approach God only as love, or we approach Him only in His love, then it is easy to view life with a minimizing view of sin. People say or think things like, God loves me, and so it is okay for

42

me to sin. With this type of approach we have not dealt with our sin; and we have missed the cleansing power of salvation.

But, if when dealing with sin, we come to God as the God who is also light, things are different. The obvious function of light is to reveal things as they are. Light does not force its way on to anyone, but you cannot lie to light. In the dark you may not know what you have kicked with your foot, but when the light is on you see what you hit.

God is light and He shines on us and reveals things, just as they are in His sight. This is what we need to properly deal with sin. When we come to God and have His light shine on our sin, we do not write off our sin as something not important or not to worry about. If we walk in the light, we see our sin as sin. In the light, we see sin as evil, and that it must be dealt with as God directs. We see that sin breaks God's heart. Seen properly, we can repent of our sin. Then we can have fellowship and enjoy the love of God, because the blood of Jesus Christ cleanses us from all sin.

This is the message which we have heard from Him and declare to you, that God is light and in Him is no darkness at all. If we say that we have fellowship with Him, and walk in darkness, we lie and do not practice the truth. But if we walk in the light as He is in the light, we have fellowship with one another, and the blood of Jesus Christ His Son cleanses us from all sin. If we say that we have no sin, we deceive ourselves, and the truth is not in us. If we confess our sins, He is faithful and just to forgive us our sins and to cleanse us from all unrighteousness. If we say that we have not sinned, we make Him a liar, and His word is not in us.

1 John 1:5-10 (NKJV)

Please note that there are some choices here. Sometimes people choose to walk in darkness. In John chapter three, we see this clearly. Men love the darkness rather than light. People also choose to be hypocrites, they say they have fellowship with God, but really walk in darkness. Either way they do not have the revelation of sin. They do not have God's light shining on their sin, revealing it for what it is. For them sin is an anti-social act, an inconvenience, a disability, or one of the other things people falsely label sin.

With a false label on sin, society runs around seeking to deal with hindrances to brotherhood, furthering human progress and the good of society, further educating people, and a plethora of do good schemes, for fixing our woes instead of seeking God's solution. Man's plans and solutions attempt to look at man and without the light and they miss the real solution to their problems.

> *And this is the condemnation, that the light has come into the world, and men loved darkness rather than light, because their deeds were evil. For everyone practicing evil hates the light and does not come to the light, lest his deeds should be exposed. But he who does the truth comes to the light, that his deeds may be clearly seen, that they have been done in God.*
>
> JOHN 3:19-21 (NKJV)

Without the light of God and His dealings with the issue of sin, all of man's plans, schemes, and programs are a waste. They miss the key to the problems and the real solution. God's light shines on the problem, declares it for what it is, sin, and opens the door for the cleansing of the blood of Jesus Christ, the only real solution to man's problems.

As men and women of prayer, the application of the revelation and truth that God is light, is twofold. First we must experience and know

God as light in our own life. We must have the cleansing power of Jesus Christ deal with our sins. This comes only from walking in the light.

If we pray without His light and its working in us, we are just do-gooders attempting to work our program and policies. We are like any other manmade programs, seeking our solutions to the problems of self and the world around us. We are devoid of understanding and power. However, if we walk in the light, including in our prayer life, then we can be an instrument of real and effective change.

The second application is for our prayers; it is imperative that our prayers include asking for light. Too many of our prayers are for things. We have compassion and so we want things for people. People need light far more than things. With light they can have life and can be successful in that life. Without light they will fail, even if they have all the things in the world.

Just as that taillight was important for me driving in Croatia, people need the light and we need to pray they will have it. People need light for salvation and for all the rest of their doings. They need light for guidance, for dealing with sin, for searching for a job, for living, for working, and for every aspect of life.

We need to pray for light. For the politician, they need light, to see a need and source for salvation, and also to see how to govern as God directs. For the pauper they need light, to see a need and source for salvation and to see God's provision for their life. For the addict they need light, to see a need and source for salvation and to see God's deliverance from death and destruction. For the unwed mother, struggling to keep her family going, she needs light, to see a need and source for salvation, for her family and herself, and for guidance and provision from God. For the missionary reaching out to a nation, he or she needs light, to see a need and source for salvation, and for seeing doors open for opportunities for the Gospel to penetrate the darkness. For the worker in the office, he or she needs light, to see a need and source for salvation, and for seeing the direction for work and service. For the business owner, he or she needs light, to see a need and source for salvation, and to see the route for the company and for leading the organization.

With light we can have fellowship with God and in that fellowship there is great and overwhelming blessing. It is this blessing we need and we should seek in praying for others and for us. In the light there is forgiveness of sin, cleansing and fellowship with God. In His fellowship there is an anointing and the overflowing cup of his goodness and mercy. Let us pray for light!

Let us pray!

Article 7

TWISTED THINKING

I n the late 1950s the best thing in the world was a package of bubblegum with baseball cards. What is not to like; I liked bubblegum and I loved baseball. Each package had a piece of gum and several cards of star baseball players. To get a card of Mickey Mantle, Roger Maris, Whitey Ford, or Yogi Berra was a wonderful prize. These may be just names to you, but they were great players on my favorite team.

One summer day, I was at Safeway and saw the packages of baseball cards. I wanted the cards. I "had to have them"; so I took them. The next thing I remember was sitting in the office of the manager of the store, waiting for my parents. I knew I had done wrong and was in big trouble. I had to face the manager and my parents; a double hitter of doom.

Even at that young age, I knew that taking the cards was wrong, but somehow I thought that since I wanted them so bad, I was entitled to take them. The next few minutes were bad enough to put an end to taking things and I have not taken baseball cards (or anything else) from stores since then.

Now I know that this trip into the sordid life of my younger years, has shocked some of you, but I mention it to get us thinking about wrong thinking or as I like to call it, twisted thinking. In my twisted thinking I thought that I deserved the gum and cards; so I could just take them.

This is not true and it is not true about bubblegum cards or anything else in life. It is twisted thinking.

We live in a time when many people justify their actions, like I did, by twisted thinking. When I was in that store, I knew it was wrong to steal, but I came to the point where I thought I was justified to steal and believed it was okay to take the cards. This was twisted thinking. It may be just a little thing or something bigger, but as long as our thinking is twisted, we will have bad results in what we do. And if there is no change in our thinking, we will validate our twisted logic to the point that we can justify anything.

Most of the time twisted thinking is not so clear and obviously wrong, like me taking those cards; often the twists hide behind good intentions and hidden agendas. The most powerful twists of thinking contain some portion of truth or a semblance of what is right. Satan used this; he tried to get Jesus to use twisted thinking, when he tempted Jesus just after Jesus' time in the wilderness. Satan quoted Scripture; all of his "If you are" statements come from the Scriptures, but then Satan added a twist away from what was right.

Walking in the twisted thinking of life, the world, Satan, or self, takes us away from faith and the abundant life promised by Jesus. In the twist, we find the thief at work and failure the result. A book could be written looking at ways we walk the twist instead of the truth, but for this article let us look just at one example where this twist/truth struggle affects answers to prayers.

> *Let us therefore come boldly to the throne of grace, that we may obtain mercy and find grace to help in time of need.*
>
> HEBREWS 4:16 (NKJV)

This is one of those powerful Scriptures on prayer, God has included in His Word. He has made provision for us to come to the throne of grace to obtain help. The word, boldly, used here, means to be outspoken, frank, and by implication speaking with assurance.

Queen Ester came to the throne room with great fear and trepidation; it was merely with the wave of a hand of the king that she would lose her life and yet she came. We, on the other hand, are told and assured, that we can come to God without fear; we have a standing invitation to come and receive. This is the promise of God and is part of the platform for effective fervent prayer that avails much.

The twist is that we take the word "bold" and use worldly practices. Bold in the world claims that you have a "right" to whatever you want, even if it is bad or evil. This twist is like my parents arriving at the office of the manager of the store and telling him to give me the bubblegum cards. It is like them trying to explain that I should have the cards, even though I did not buy them, because I wanted them.

In worldly thinking, boldness in prayer is going to God and demanding that He give me what I want; whatever I want, how and when I want it. It is demanding anything I come up with, in my twists of thinking. The twists of the world, of Satan, or of self, bring problems and it does not move God, because it does not come by faith. The results of twisted thinking and demanding are always destructive.

By contrast, the promises of God, walked out as He directs and commands bring good results. We are to come boldly to His throne. His promise is there for those who will follow His direction and command. We are to come boldly to the throne, His way, and not allow twisted thinking.

The key word here is the untwisted meaning of the word, "boldly". It means to come to the throne with assurance. The twisted way is self-assurance or worldly assurance, either of these, are weak and negative. A far better way, God's way, is to have the assurance of God. This assurance brings boldness, far superior and much more productive, than anything the world can bring.

Effective prayer comes from boldness in prayer; and godly boldness comes from placing our body as a living sacrifice, on the altar, giving our self to God. Derek Prince has several wonderful teaching on the reasonable service of the living sacrifice. Here is an example:

> "Once you have placed your body on God's altar in total surrender, your body no longer belongs to you. It belongs to God. You no longer decide what happens to your body. God does. You do not determine what kind of job you are going to do with your body. God does. You do not choose where you are going to live. God does. But it is wonderful when He takes the responsibility."

Living sacrifice is presenting our body to God. When God takes responsibility He brings changes. He ends conformity to the world and its ways, He transforms our mind, and causes us to know His will. His changes destroy twists of thinking and provides for bold prayer. You can be assured in prayer, when God has taken responsibility? Yes!

> *I beseech you therefore, brethren, by the mercies of God, that you present your bodies a living sacrifice, holy, acceptable to God, which is your reasonable service. And do not be conformed to this world, but be transformed by the renewing of your mind, that you may prove what is that good and acceptable and perfect will of God.*
>
> ROMANS 12:1-2 (NKJV)

The demands of self are always twisted; the demands of sacrifice are sweet to God. We come to Him on His terms, pray His will and His prayers. And when we pray this way, we can expect His wonderful, powerful answers.

On the altar of living sacrifice, we can boldly bring our prayers. When there is less of me, there is room for more of Him. And He is more loving, more knowledgeable, more caring and wise; His prayers are better than anything we have ever dreamed of praying, so why come in our own boldness with our prayers, when we can come with His.

Today, He is offering a place on the altar, a special place for you and me. From this place He promises to untwist, guide, and direct us, so our prayers are His prayers and result in great blessing. Let us come boldly to the throne of grace.

Let us pray!

Article 8

IN THE NEIGHBORHOOD

For me the mid to late 1950s was a time of great fun and excitement. Growing up I had many wonderful advantages; my family loved me and cared for me and my neighborhood was filled with great friends, and lots of fun. My friend Donnie's house was down the street. They had a great house and yard and there was always something fun happening there. At the other end of the street was Geno's house. His dad had a new Chevy and Geno and I drove that car to California—all from the safety of his driveway.

Across the street was Jeff's house, playing with Jeff was great fun and his mom made cookies! One day I walked into their kitchen as she was baking chocolate chip cookies. There were dozens and dozens of cookies cooling on every flat surface of the kitchen. Think of this, I am about five years old and everywhere you looked all you could see was cookies!

There were many fun times growing up in this neighborhood. Mr. Kissler took a walk every afternoon and he liked to give kids candy. There was a swimming pool just a few blocks from our house. Every summer another friend of mine, Matt, had older brothers who would come home for the summer.

One summer we built a fort in Matt's back yard. The first step was to dig an eight foot by eight foot square and eight feet deep hole. We then covered this hole with heavy planks of wood, covered the wood with plastic, and then dirt. To get into the fort we dug straight down, a few feet from the main hole and then tunneled into the fort. Even though I was the youngest boy there, they let me dig part of the tunnel. They lowered me into the hole and I would fill a bucket with dirt and they would pull it up. This was great fun!

I lived in a great neighborhood, but in the Bible there is an invitation to enjoy something even better. In the Gospel of John, we are invited to walk in the love of Jesus and to keep His Word. If we do, then Jesus and the Father will come and make their home with us. Wow, Jesus and the Father living at my house. Now that is a great neighborhood!

> *Jesus answered and said to him, "If anyone loves Me, he will keep My word; and My Father will love him, and We will come to him and make Our home with him.*
>
> JOHN 14:23 (NKJV)

In a modern paraphrase of the Bible called *The Message*, by Eugene Peterson, he writes, **"If anyone loves me, he will carefully keep my word and my Father will love him—we'll move right into the neighborhood!"**

Can you imagine what this would be like? Think what people would say, "Guess who is living in the neighborhood?" This would change things in almost every neighborhood; in some neighborhoods this would make for a radical change. And many of our neighborhoods could use a radical change. What difference would it make if Jesus and the Father moved in with you? What would change?

How would things change, if every day, when you awoke, Jesus was there at your kitchen table waiting for you? What if when you went for a walk, Jesus was ready and willing to walk with you? What if every time you left to go to work, Jesus was waiting to carpool with you? What if He was standing there listening to all of your conversations? What if when you picked a movie, Jesus was there reading the reviews and making suggestions? What if every time you sat down to watch TV, Jesus was sitting with you? Would there be a difference in how you talked, worked, acted, and prayed?

If Jesus is Lord of your life, then He is there with you, but too often people live as though He and the Father are far away. Living with Jesus and the Father in our home, daily walking with Them, would, for most people, bring many radical changes. These would be great changes and would bring great benefits to the man or woman involved.

> *Abide in Me, and I in you. As the branch cannot bear fruit of itself, unless it abides in the vine, neither can you, unless you abide in Me. I am the vine, you are the branches. He who abides in Me, and I in him, bears much fruit; for without Me you can do nothing.*
>
> JOHN 15:4-5 (NKJV)

> *If you abide in Me, and My words abide in you, you will ask what you desire, and it shall be done for you. By this My Father is glorified, that you bear much fruit; so you will be My disciples.*
>
> JOHN 15:7-8 (NKJV)

In a close and constant walk with Jesus and the Father, we grow and mature, we build our faith, we walk in love, we serve as servants, we minister in power, and we can have great power in prayer. This is the true source of effectiveness in life, ministry, and prayer.

In John chapter 15 this walk is called, abiding. Abiding with Christ is the secret for success of the men and women who have done great things in Christ. They learned to abide and made the changes necessary to continue to abide. They made abiding a priority over everything else in their life. Habits and lifestyle were changed and things were given up, all for the sake of being with Jesus and the Father, everyday, all day, even when they were working at other things.

The power of abiding is still available to Christians today. Those who learn to abide and make arrangements so they can continue to abide, and by abiding do exploits. Most Christians long for this kind of relationship and the power that comes from abiding. The world is filled with things that are crooked, bent out of shape, twisted, backwards, upside down, and just not right. The answer to solve these problems is the work and prayers of men and women, abiding with Christ. Abider's work is valuable, their ministry is powerful, their love is sweet, their sacrifice is meaningful, their understanding is deep, their walk is straight, and their prayers are effective. This is what we want and this is what the world needs.

Abiding is available to all Christians; Jesus has already paid the price, so we can be redeemed and we can walk in a deep, constant, place of abiding with Jesus and the Father. However, abiding has a requirement. Jesus makes very clear the requirements. If a person does what Jesus says to do, then the result He has made possible, will happen. The first part of the requirement, we are to love Jesus. Loving Jesus is also to love the Father; as Jesus and the Father are together as one.

Jesus answered and said to him, "If anyone loves Me, he will keep My word; and My Father will love him, and We will come to him and make Our home with him.

JOHN 14:23 (NKJV)

You shall love the Lord your God with all your heart, with all your soul, and with all your strength.

DEUTERONOMY 6:5 (NKJV)

And now, Israel, what does the Lord your God require of you, but to fear the Lord your God, to walk in all His

ways and to love Him, to serve the Lord your God with
all your heart and with all your soul,

DEUTERONOMY 10:12 (NKJV)

The second part of the requirement is keeping God's Word. Simply put, Jesus requires of us that we show our love by obeying His Word, command, and instructions. This also includes obeying those things He tells us to do, day-by-day, by the Holy Spirit. The two requirements are tied together; we are to love and obey. If we love and obey, then we can abide. If we love and obey, then Jesus and the Father will come and make Their home with us.

'And it shall be that if you earnestly obey My
commandments which I command you today, to love the
Lord your God and serve Him with all your heart and
with all your soul,

DEUTERONOMY 11:13 (NKJV)

"Therefore whoever hears these sayings of Mine, and
does them, I will liken him to a wise man who built his
house on the rock: and the rain descended, the floods
came, and the winds blew and beat on that house;
and it did not fall, for it was founded on the rock. But
everyone who hears these sayings of Mine, and does not
do them, will be like a foolish man who built his house
on the sand: and the rain descended, the floods came,
and the winds blew and beat on that house; and it fell.
And great was its fall."

MATTHEW 7:24-27 (NKJV)

How is your neighborhood? How is the neighborhood where you live, but also the neighborhood of your heart, your family, your church, and your nation? Most need help and that help comes from the prayers and work of men and women who love and obey, so they can abide with Christ. Will you do all that you must do, so that the work of Christ can be complete in you, so you can abide?

Let us pray!

Article 9

CHARACTER AND PRAYER

When I was growing up I loved baseball, both playing and watching the game. Colorado did not have a major league team then, so I was free to pick any team to support and I liked winners, so I became a fan of the New York Yankees. This team had some wonderful players. One of the best was Mickey Mantle. Mantle could do it all, he was an outstanding fielder, very fast runner, and he could hit. He was so good that he was voted into the Hall of Fame.

Mantle died a few years ago and shortly before his death he gave an interview, in which he reminisced about the great teams and wonderful times he enjoyed as a ball player. A sad part of the interview was when he talked about all the injuries he had suffered in his career.

One of the speculations then, and one that continues today, is what kind of records and how great Mantle could have been if he had been healthy. This man was a great player, yet several seasons he only played part of the year and his overall career was cut short by injuries. In this interview and at other times, Mantle speculated as to what he could have done if he had trained well and taken care of his body. Some people believe he could have been the best baseball player of all time.

And how about you, let us speculate for a moment. In what areas are you great? And more importantly, what has God prepared for you. He has sent His Son to bring you into His Family as a member of the family and a joint heir with Christ. He has given you the Holy Spirit to walk with you, to train and guide you. He loves you with an unfading, unfailing love. He has made provision for you in His economy and plans. God has made great preparation for you; He has prepared you for greatness!

> *For we are His workmanship, created in Christ Jesus*
> *for good works, which God prepared beforehand that*
> *we should walk in them.*
> EPHESIANS 2:10 (NKJV)

However, there is always a question that must be asked and must be dealt with, one way or another. What will you do with God's preparation? This is the question that faces every man, woman, and child. God has given Jesus so you can have an abundant life, what will you do with it? For those who receive Jesus as Lord, there is salvation. For those who refuse, there is damnation.

Once you have received Jesus as Lord, then there follows a series of opportunities to deal with this same question. What else will you do with God's preparation? Will you receive the Holy Spirit and walk in His training and guidance? Will you walk as a son or daughter, walking as a joint heir with Jesus? Will you allow the fragrance of the knowledge of God flow through you to others?

> *Now thanks be to God who always leads us in triumph*
> *in Christ, and through us diffuses the fragrance of His*
> *knowledge in every place.*
> 2 CORINTHIANS 2:14 (NKJV)

These are just a few of the areas covered by the question, what will you do with God's preparation for your life? As we walk day-by-day with the Lord, we explore more of the range and possibilities of this question and learn more of how to respond. Hopefully, you are growing and maturing in your walk. Just as the pundits of sports speculate on how great Mickey Mantle could have been, so we can speculate on how great you can be in Christ.

God's expectation is that we would be like Jesus. Paul longed to know Christ and His power, so He could be like Jesus. God's preparations made a way for Paul and for us to be like Jesus. The question is will we walk in God's preparation and if so, how fully.

Here is where the speculation comes in. What has God called you to do? And what are you doing to accomplish what God has planned. At the end of your life will you be the best you could be, having done all, or will there be speculation on what you might have done?

This line of thought is very important for effective prayer. It is easy to take a road of prayer that is less than our best. Mantle was good, but he did not do the things he could, to be his best. Many people who pray today take that same road. They pray, but they do not do all they could to be their best in prayer, to be the best they can be.

Are there areas in your life that keep you from being your best? Are there areas that hinder your prayers? Are there areas that limit your prayers? To be effective in prayer, we must develop our life in a way that allows us to do things, everything, God's way.

In effective prayer there is no other way. It is truly His way or no way. Effective prayer begins with a life of faith and faith comes by the Word of God. As we spend time with the Word, and Jesus is the Word, making Him primary to our life, plans, actions, and beliefs, then we can have a depth of faith that brings great answers to prayer.

Prayers that avail much are also built on a life of love. Without love we have nothing of value and our prayers are just words, they accomplish nothing. We must love like God loves; His love is pure, overwhelming, limitless, and boundless. His love is deep, it overcomes, and it reaches out. His love is powerful and perfect. He is love and there is no shadow or turning in His love. His love is for the sinner and saint. If we are going to have effective prayers then we must come to the place where we have the love of God flowing unconditionally, fully, and purely, reaching out to all those around us, just as He does.

Faith and love are keys to great prayers, however, if we are going to be effective in prayer there is one other area important for our success; character. Our prayers are limited by our character. Our character is like the boat that carries faith and love in our prayers.

Using my example of the ball player Mickey Mantle, he had the things necessary to be a great ball player. He could run and catch, he was a wonderful batter; he had it all. However, he had not been trained and had not learned that there was more to baseball than running, catching, and hitting. His regret, spoken of in an interview late in his life, was that he had wasted his opportunities, by not doing the things off the field that he should have. This failure cost him parts of seasons, many games where he was not his best, and even shortened his career.

For the man or woman who espouses to be great in prayer, character issues are what will make or break our success. We cannot be a man or woman of prayer and walk like the world and act like the world. If our character is not strong, we will stumble and fail in prayer. And we must include all aspects of character. Look at Paul's list of some aspects of character. How do you measure up?

> *But the fruit of the Spirit is love, joy, peace, longsuffering, kindness, goodness, faithfulness, gentleness, self-control. Against such there is no law. And those who are Christ's have crucified the flesh with its passions and desires. If*

we live in the Spirit, let us also walk in the Spirit. Let us not become conceited, provoking one another, envying one another.

GALATIANS 5:22-26 (NKJV)

High expectation for prayer must be met with high attainment of character. A broken character, where aspects of good character are not present, will limit our prayers, our usefulness in prayer, and our greatness in prayer. We are fooling ourselves if we think we can pray like a saint and live like a devil. We are sorely mistaken if we think we can have faith to move mountains, but live with a character of darkness.

God is calling for men and women who will pray, and He is working to make us men and women of character, so we can pray effectively.

For you were once darkness, but now you are light in the Lord. Walk as children of light (for the fruit of the Spirit is in all goodness, righteousness, and truth), finding out what is acceptable to the Lord.

EPHESIANS 5:8-10 (NKJV)

If we are going to be effective in prayer we must build our character. We must be more and more like Jesus. We must know Jesus, His power, His fellowship, and His death. This is the high calling of God for us in Christ Jesus. The man or woman, who seeks after Jesus and to be like Him in all things and at all times, will pray like Him.

For the grace of God that brings salvation has appeared to all men, teaching us that, denying ungodliness and worldly lusts, we should live soberly, righteously, and godly in the present age, looking for the blessed hope and glorious appearing of our great God and Savior Jesus

Christ, who gave Himself for us, that He might redeem us from every lawless deed and purify for Himself His own special people, zealous for good works.

TITUS 2:11-14 (NKJV)

Let us pray!

Unit Two

PASSION FOR
EFFECTIVE PRAYER

M y Grandma sat in the living room of her cabin near Estes Park
on July 31, 1976 and watched the Big Thompson Canyon Flood
flow past her window. It had rained 12 inches in less than 4 hours and
around 9 p.m. a 20 foot wall of water raced down the canyon. The water
came closer and closer to her cabin. Throughout the night the water
ravaged the area destroying more than 400 cars and 400 houses, taking
the lives of more than 140 people.

Grandma was okay, she was rescued the next day. After placing
Grandma, her suitcase, and a few items in the Jeep, the rescue party
drove out the driveway of her house. The only problem was that the
flood had taken out part of the yard and driveway. The water covering
the end of the driveway was not a few inches deep as they assumed,
but several feet. The jeep flipped and threw Grandma into the river. She
almost drowned being rescued!

My Grandma not only lived there, but also had a gift shop. The
flood had not touched her cabin, but it had gone through her shop,
leaving three feet of mud everywhere. Many of the storage cabinets

were now completely filled with mud. The task of recovery seemed overwhelming.

Then the Mennonites arrived. This is a group of Mennonites who go to disasters like this and help with the cleanup. They have a passion for helping people. They began to dig out the mud and wash walls, cabinets, shelves, tables, and floors. They provided meals, comfort, and support. I do not know what my Grandma would have done, but with their help, she was able to reopen her shop.

I worked with a man who was passionate everything he did. He had been a Marine and I knew him as a football (American football) coach. He loved every aspect of football, especially winning. We coached the junior varsity team together. At the beginning of the year the team was terrible. After one of the losses he said, "That is enough." and called a special practice and that is when his passion came out.

He was all over the practice field talking to everyone, pushing boys to work harder. He did not yell, but he was so passionate that everyone responded; even the other coaches were better. By the end of the practice we were ready to win and we did not lose another game the rest of the year!

This is what we need in prayer, passion. The Mennonites used their passion to help people all over the country. This coach used passion to make young people into winners. And passion can change our prayer life and prayers.

God has told us and repeatedly demonstrated that He is willing and able to answer prayers. If we do what He has said to do, He has committed to do what He has promised. Passion in prayer seizes the opportunity; receiving answers to our prayers. Effective prayer requires more than just a longing for answers, it must have passion.

Do you have a passion for answers to your prayers? Passion is caught. It comes from drawing close to a source. Our source for passion in prayer is Jesus. Jesus was so passionate about His love for mankind that He gave Himself. Jesus is also passionate about the success of our prayer life. He has chosen to make His passion for prayer available for men and women to catch. If we will draw near to Him, His passion will leap into our hearts and burn bright, causing a passion for prayer that will transform our prayers from ritual to resolve.

Let us pray!

God's plan for prayer includes men and women with a passion for effective prayer. He works with sons and daughters who are willing to be used as vessels for His Kingdom work, prepared for effective prayer and wonderful answers from God, and filled with passion. The articles of Unit Two—*Passion for Effective Prayer*, focus on making our passion, effective fervent prayer that avails much.

Article 10

UP TO . . .

I enjoy teaching, and while it could have its moments, generally, it is a great profession. The best part of teaching was the young people. They can be bizarre and frustrating, and then the next moment they can be wonderful; mature beyond their years, full of excitement, promise, and compassion. They live in a strange situation; exploring self and the world. They fight for individuality, by rigidly conforming to the norms of their peers. So every day in a high school is an adventure.

Most of the time high school students make you very proud. They do many things right, they can be compassionate, they overcome difficult obstacles, and they often excel beyond expectations. At other times they know far more than they live up to, and often so do we.

One of the most frustrating things for our Heavenly Father must be our failure to live up to our potential. God has provided a new life for us, a life beyond compare, and most of us, often fail to live up to all we could be, in Christ. Habitually, we live life on a standard far below what God has prepared for us; limiting blessings and opportunities. He has made provision for His children to walk on the earth as giants; for us to be conquerors, to walk like Jesus, as He walked the earth. Jesus said we would do what He did and more, however, most people live far short of this. We fall short on accomplishments and far below His standards.

Most assuredly, I say to you, he who believes in Me, the works that I do he will do also; and greater works than these he will do, because I go to My Father.

JOHN 14:12 (NKJV)

Yet in all these things we are more than conquerors through Him who loved us.

ROMANS 8:37 (NKJV)

And while most people live below God's planned standard, no generation has known more. Bibles are available everywhere and are available in many formats and every device of technology. Study is so easy, with a couple of clicks we can have a list of every time a word appears in the Bible. We can compare verses in five or ten translations, or we can see the meaning of Hebrew or Greek words from early versions of the Bible. We can listen to the Bible or even have it presented with multiple actors playing the roles of the people. And with thousands of Bible helps, aides, magazines, and websites, we can know more than ever. So today there is even more we should live up to and do.

In my classroom, I would work with students, telling them that with some work they could be successful. However, sometimes students would not even do a little. How often the Father tries to get us to learn and use His Word to live the good life He has prepared. God has prepared a wonderful life for us to walk in, but so often we walk in the ways of the world and suffer the consequences. There is so much more to life that the world's ways. We should be living a life of great victory and power, and yet we are living up to so little.

Paul saw this problem in his day; Christians were not living up to what they knew. The revelation of Christ found in the Paul's epistles is of an abundant life in Christ Jesus. This life is a victory over destruction and death. It is a life of great power, with answers to prayer that astonish even the most hardhearted person. It is a life of fellowship with the

Father, Son, and Holy Sprit, and with men and women here on earth that is sweet and fulfilling. And yet Paul saw people not living up to what they knew.

> *Not that I have already attained, or am already*
> *perfected; but I press on, that I may lay hold of that for*
> *which Christ Jesus has also laid hold of me.*
> PHILIPPIANS 3:12 (NKJV)

In the *God's Word* translation the last part of this verse is translated, *"But I run to win that which Jesus Christ has already won for me."* Jesus has won a wonderful victory for us, giving us the opportunity to walk with Him far beyond anything the world has known. But we must run to win what Jesus has won for us.

Shortly after the resurrection of Christ, we saw Paul and a few other Christians, turn the world right side up; conquering hearts and minds for Jesus from one end of the Mediterranean to the other. This small band of men and women went from a 120 people in the upper room, to a worldwide force, in just a few years. What God did with and through these people was not even unimaginable because it was so improbable. And yet they did it.

Not living up to what we know, is a major problem today. Maybe it would be better to write this as, not living up to what we should know. There is a gap between what people know and do, but that gap is made wider because there is also a gap between what we know and what we should know. This causes many a Christian life to fall far short of expectation and this is a shortfall even with a commonly held very low expectation of what the Christian life should and could be.

Jesus taught about living up to what we know in Matthew chapter twenty-five. In the story of the three men given talents, two worked with the talents and earned more. The other man hid the money he was given. We know the story and that the man who gave the talents, was well pleased with the work of the first two and angry with the third man.

Please take note of the third man and what he said. *Then he who had received the one talent came and said, "Lord, I knew you to be a hard man, reaping where you have not sown, and gathering where you have not scattered seed".* This man claimed to know the man who gave the talents, but look at the story; this third man, did not know what he was talking about. The man, giving the talents, gave talents; the Greek word denotes a sum of money, and when he returned, the original sum of money, plus the increase, was given to the first two men, with the *"Well done good and faithful servant . . ."* The talent giving man was is was a most generous man.

Instead of knowing God as He has revealed Himself in the Bible, most people are satisfied with illusion and misrepresentation. Much of what they know is incomplete or just plain wrong. How like the third man, are most people; assuming they know God, His promises, and plans, but only knowing their assumptions.

Jesus, the author of our faith, is also the finisher, not of our "get by" or "do a little", but finisher of running fully, completely, and successfully, the race set before us. The talents He gives are not lesser or greater than those given to another, but are perfect for us and our race of life.

> *Therefore we also, since we are surrounded by so great a cloud of witnesses, let us lay aside every weight, and the sin which so easily ensnares us, and let us run with endurance the race that is set before us, looking unto Jesus, the author and finisher of our faith, who for the joy that was set before Him endured the cross, despising the shame, and has sat down at the right hand of the throne of God.*
>
> HEBREWS 12:1-2 (NKJV)

In addition, and this is very important, we need to remember that our dealings with God are supernatural. He is not limited by the natural. The talents He gives to Christians are not just natural abilities or talents, but go far beyond. For too long we have tried to live our Christian life just in the natural; more like the third man, than the first two. The talents given to Christians go far beyond the talents of our natural ability. When Jesus ascended into heaven, He gave to us His Name, His authority, and His power.

> *And He said to them, "Go into all the world and preach the gospel to every creature. He who believes and is baptized will be saved; but he who does not believe will be condemned. And these signs will follow those who believe: In My name they will cast out demons; they will speak with new tongues; they will take up serpents; and if they drink anything deadly, it will by no means hurt them; they will lay hands on the sick, and they will recover."*
>
> MARK 16:15-18 (NKJV)

> *But you shall receive power when the Holy Spirit has come upon you; and you shall be witnesses to Me in Jerusalem, and in all Judea and Samaria, and to the end of the earth.*
>
> ACTS 1:8 (NKJV)

What are we going to do with the talents Jesus has given us? He has given us the use of His name. This is not just tag on to the end of our prayers, but the use of the most powerful name in the universe. We have authority to pray just as if Jesus was standing with us praying. We are His ambassadors, here on assignment, with the full use of His name. Will we use this "talent" or hide it?

It's not that I've already reached the goal or have already completed the course. But I run to win that which Jesus Christ has already won for me.

PHILIPPIANS 3:12 (GOD'S WORD)

Let us pray!

I AM . . .

F or many years I taught in the same high school; it was a good
school, but we experienced a regular change of principals. Some
of the changes, in the early years were due to the poor job of the person
in the position. However, for most of the time, the regular turnover of
principals was due to the transfer of a great principal to a school that was
in desperate needed of help.

This meant that many years when the school year began, we had
a new principal. With each of the new principals came a new call for
excellence. The steady stream of new principals, diverse in many ways, all
had one thing in common; they had ideas on how to make a school better.
None of these principals were the type of people satisfied with the way
things were. We even had a person fill in for just one term, knowing that
she would be there only one term and then retire, but even this principal
sought to bring about changes to make the school better.

With each new principal, all of us on the staff would roll our eyes
and say, "Here we go again." We knew we were a good school, but these
principals were never satisfied; all they could see was that there were
areas where we could be better. And these principals had the drive to
work for change. They would present what they wanted to accomplish
and slowly, often with dragging heals of the staff, we would come to see

that these changes he or she wanted to implement were important and what we needed. We would realize that we had become complacent in "begin a good school". And slowly we would work through the process and become better.

Generally people like complacency; it is a desired and natural state. From Adam to me, history is filled with the testimony, by word and deed, of men moving to a place of complacency. This is true in people, but also in the great moves of man, time and again the fire and fervor of a move of God has cooled and the people have become complacent. Too often complacency has cooled revival fires. Too often complacency has cooled mission outreaches. Too often complacency has stolen workers and funds from good works. Too often complacency has quieted preaching. Too often complacency has silenced the voice of prayer.

Jesus was well aware of this nature of slipping into complacency in man, read carefully the story of the prodigal son. Often the story is used in preaching to sinners, but note it also has application to those who are already sons of the Father. Note the life, words, and actions of the older bother. Surely he was a type of the complacent Christian, who never transgressed, yet never possessed his possessions. The person who never accomplishes what he or she could do in Christ.

> *And he said to him, 'Your brother has come, and because he has received him safe and sound, your father has killed the fatted calf.' But he was angry and would not go in. Therefore his father came out and pleaded with him. So he answered and said to his father, 'Lo, these many years I have been serving you; I never transgressed your commandment at any time; and yet you never gave me a young goat, that I might make merry with my friends. But as soon as this son of yours came, who has devoured your livelihood with harlots, you killed the fatted calf*

*for him.' And he said to him, 'Son, you are always with
me, and all that I have is yours.*

LUKE 15:27-31 (NKJV)

More obvious and to the point, is the problem of complacency given
to us in the letter to the church in Laodicea, found in the third chapter
of the book of Revelations. The Laodiceans are described as lukewarm,
neither cold nor hot. This is a very good description of complacency. The
Laodiceans were much like the older brother; blind to their condition
and unwilling to possess what they had in Christ.

It is clear from the letter to this church that the state of lukewarm or
complacent is very dangerous. The Lord wants all of us to be hot; on fire
for Him and the things of the Kingdom. To be lukewarm is so dangerous
that the Lord would even prefer a person be cold over being lukewarm.
Remember the prodigal son was cold (very cold), but he finally came to
his senses and returned to his father.

*"And to the angel of the church of the Laodiceans
write, 'These things says the Amen, the Faithful and
True Witness, the Beginning of the creation of God: I
know your works, that you are neither cold nor hot. I
could wish you were cold or hot. So then, because you
are lukewarm, and neither cold nor hot, I will vomit
you out of My mouth. Because you say, 'I am rich, have
become wealthy, and have need of nothing'—and do not
know that you are wretched, miserable, poor, blind, and
naked—'"*

REVELATION 3:14-22 (NKJV)

One of the elements of complacency that makes it so dangerous is
that it is subtle. It comes into a person quietly, without fanfare and settles
into one area or more in a person's life. The Lord described complacency

of the Laodiceans as, "Because you say, I am . . . and do not know . . ." Complacency is most often a false sense of who we are and the nature of our life, beliefs, and action. We think one thing, when reality is another. They thought they were doing well, but the Lord knew they were, wretched, miserable, poor, blind, and naked.

This letter was written to the church at Laodicea, but it has been given to Christians for two thousand years, as a warning to avoid complacency and to be on guard for dealing with the evils of this condition when it strikes. As long as Satan is around and doing his best to kill, steal, and destroy, there will be a danger of complacency. Everyone who desires to go on with God, and fulfill his or her calling in Christ, must guard against and deal with complacency.

This is especially true of people who long to be effective in prayer. How easy it is for prayers to become lukewarm, prayers that are neither hot nor cold. How often have our prayers been wretched, miserable, poor, blind, and naked? How often has the High Priest of our Confession, the Lord Jesus Christ, had to spit our prayers out of his mouth? All because we were complacent and our prayers were lukewarm. How often have we said, I am rich in prayers, wealthy in my prayer life, but have nothing to show for my pretense of prayer and claims of fruit?

The Laodiceans made three claims, do we make these claims as well. First they said, "I am rich". They laid claim to the riches found in Christ, but did not live in those riches. Arthur Wallis in his book, *In the Day of Thy Power*, describes their claim as,

> "They made much of the great objective side of truth—without realizing that such is vain unless backed up by the subjective or experimental side. In other words, it was no use talking about being spiritual millionaires while they were living like spiritual paupers. It was no use congratulating each other that they were blessed "with every spiritual blessing . . . in

Christ" or that they were "in everything . . . enriched in
him" if they were manifestly not living in the good of
their inheritance."

Second they talked of their spiritual increase, "I . . . have become
wealthy". They did not understand, the wealth given to them by Christ
was true wealth, but it is given not to brag about, or for a person to rest
on his or her laurels, it is to be invested and to increase. The third man
given talents in Jesus parable, was rejected because he was not profitable
using the talent given. Wallis writes, "Light obeyed will increase".

Third the Laodiceans claimed, their spiritual independence, they
said, "I . . . have need of nothing". They were not hungry for the things of
God, because they did not see a need; they believed that they knew it all
and they had it all. Wallis describes their attitude,

> "Did someone suggest an extra church prayer meeting
> to implore God's blessing? They had no need of such
> a thing. Was mention made of a day to be set apart for
> humiliation and confession in view of the prevailing
> deadness? It was quite uncalled for—things were going
> well. Was concern expressed that the gospel service was
> not reaching the people or resulting in conversion? The
> gospel service had always been quite adequate, and the
> results must be left with God. Did someone dare to
> suggest that there was a suspicion of coldness in the
> service of worship? The gatherings were all that could
> be desired."

Are the claims of the Laodiceans, our claims? Does Jesus see us as
wretched, miserable, poor, blind, and naked?

For the Laodiceans, and equally for us, Christ offers an answer to
complacency. We can buy of Him gold refined by fire. The spiritual

blessings we need are still available to us. To those who hunger and thirst, Christ is ready and able to bring food and drink. Christ advises that we buy true spiritual gold so they will be rich in faith. He councils white garments of the righteousness of Christ, seen in a practical outworking day by day. He directs for blindness eye salve to anoint their eyes; to see, to really see with the eyes of our understanding being enlightened.

> *that the God of our Lord Jesus Christ, the Father of glory, may give to you the spirit of wisdom and revelation in the knowledge of Him, the eyes of your understanding being enlightened; that you may know what is the hope of His calling, what are the riches of the glory of His inheritance in the saints.*
>
> EPHESIANS 1:17-18 (NKJV)

> *If then you were raised with Christ, seek those things which are above, where Christ is, sitting at the right hand of God.*
>
> COLOSSIANS 3:1 (NKJV)

Remember that school I mentioned at the beginning of this article? It was a good school, but there were areas were we had grown complacent. The new principal would challenge us and work with us to bring about change so we could be better.

The Principal of our life, our Heavenly Father, is challenging us today, to work with Him and come up to His standard of faith and trust, of work and prayer. The Lord is standing at our door; He has come in love, seeking those who will repent of complacency and anything that would hinder their effectual working in the Body of Christ. He is knocking, will we hear his knock, will we recognize our need for Him, and will we let Him in? Will we seek to live fully in the fullness of His righteousness and life?

> *"I counsel you to buy from Me gold refined in the fire, that you may be rich; and white garments, that you may be clothed, that the shame of your nakedness may not be revealed; and anoint your eyes with eye salve, that you may see. As many as I love, I rebuke and chasten. Therefore be zealous and repent. Behold, I stand at the door and knock. If anyone hears My voice and opens the door, I will come in to him and dine with him, and he with Me. To him who overcomes I will grant to sit with Me on My throne, as I also overcame and sat down with My Father on His throne. He who has an ear, let him hear what the Spirit says to the churches."*
>
> REVELATION 3:18-22 (NKJV)

Let us pray!

Article 12

TAKING OUR PLACE

E veryone was there, the elders, the religious leaders, the movers and shakers, Jesse and his family, and Samuel. And most importantly, Samuel had come with the anointing oil of God. This would be a memorable day; the anointing of the new king. For Jesse, his son, Eliab, would be king. For the elders of the town, prestige and honor of the king coming from their town, not to mention the influence they would have in the government and the increase of their prestige and status. So it was no surprise that everyone was so excited.

With great anticipation, everyone gathered to watch. Samuel called for Jesse's oldest son Eliab; here was the moment they all were waiting for. Samuel and the horn of anointing oil, and . . .

What do you mean, "This is not the one?"

"Ah, well there is the second son, Abinadab. He also looks like a king; he will make a fine leader for the people".

"This is not the one??"

"Shammah?"

"This is not the one???"

"And . . . and . . . and . . . and . . . , well, there is one other son." "There is David, but he is out keeping the sheep". "Send for him."

Can you imagine what it was like, as the people, Jesse and his family, the elders of the town, the religious leaders, and everyone else, stood around waiting for the servant to go and get David? Talk about your uncomfortable silences. Everyone was embarrassed, think of the seven sons of Jesse, all having been refused for the position. Can you imagine what the people were thinking?

You know the rest of the story. Samuel anointed David to be king. God had stopped Samuel from anointing Eliab and his brothers because God does not look at the appearance or the stature of the man. God looks at the heart. And the heart God was searching for was David's.

> *So it was, when they came, that he looked at Eliab and said, "Surely the Lord's anointed is before Him." But the Lord said to Samuel, "Do not look at his appearance or at the height of his stature, because I have refused him. For the Lord does not see as man sees; for man looks at the outward appearance, but the Lord looks at the heart."*
>
> 1 SAMUEL 16:6-7 (NKJV)

How about today? How often is the life of Christians, church services, prayer meetings, and even special events, like the time when the seven sons of Jesse were not selected to be king? Samuel was there ready to anoint, but the anointing oil remained in the horn. Often our life, work, and ministry, is carried out on our own strength, power, and tradition; instead of empowered and directed by the Holy Spirit?

Are our activities anointed with the Holy Spirit or just the outward appearance of meeting with God? Has our life become so set in our ways and plans that we can do without God and the Holy Spirit? Could it be that our meetings are so well planed and presented, with special music and skilled musicians, gifted speakers, and trained helpers, to cover for a lack of the anointing? How often do our meetings resemble the awkward time when the seven brothers were rejected, instead of the glorious time when Samuel poured out the anointing oil on David?

The anointing of David, as was true with the anointing of the judges and other kings of the Old Testament, gave power to the man to deliver and lead Israel. The oil that was poured on the man is a type, or picture, of the Holy Spirit. It was the power of God for the man.

Today under the New Covenant, the better covenant in Christ, the anointing of the Holy Spirit is available to us. This anointing is what changes men to disciples, disciples who share their life and the Word, with power. This anointing is what changes church meetings from something like a social club to meetings honoring God and His Word, and are filled with the power of the Holy Spirit.

> *So Samuel took the horn of oil and anointed him in the presence of his brothers, and from that day on the Spirit of the Lord came upon David in power.*
>
> 1 SAMUEL 16:13 (NIV)

I do not mean to condemn us, our meetings, or practices, but it would be good for us to check ourselves and our meetings. What do our meetings most closely resemble, the uncomfortable time of when the seven sons of Jesse were rejected, or the glorious coming of the power of God, when Samuel anointed David? Christianity is not about the appearance or the stature, but the heart. Too many Christians and too many churches have lost the power of the anointing and the change of heart that goes with it. Their life and work is filled with activity, often they are very busy with activity, but without the power of the anointing.

WHAT ABOUT YOUR HEART?

The key for David was his heart. The key for us, today, is our heart. It is the prepared heart that opens the door for God to work with and through a Christian. The Word of God is very powerful and sown in good soil of a heart it will produce a great crop.

> *Break up your fallow ground, for it is time to seek the*
> *Lord, till He comes and rains righteousness on you.*
>
> HOSEA 10:12 (NKJV)

The process presented here is simple. Step one; break up the fallow ground, this is heart preparation. Step two; seek the Lord, this is effective prayer. Step three; continue until the result comes, God's rain of righteousness. This process has been powerful and effective in the life of Christians for centuries and it is the perfect prescription for men and women who long to be effective, especially in prayer.

The responsibility is yours. This is a stumbling block for many people; they are waiting for God. However, this command, like others in the Bible, is God directing us to go and do. God has done the greater part already. He has brought a great redemption to man through Christ Jesus, opening the door for a full and complete salvation. This gives us the right and power to walk as Jesus walked; in the anointing of the Holy Spirit, with life changing force available for our life and to help those in need.

> *But sanctify the Lord God in your hearts, and always*
> *be ready to give a defense to everyone who asks you a*
> *reason for the hope that is in you, with meekness and*
> *fear;*
>
> 1 PETER 3:15 (NKJV)

"Breaking up the fallow ground" of our heart means to bring them to a humble and contrite state before God. It is only with the man or woman who has come to God in this manner, who will be prepared.

Among the most common and most destructive sins hindering this is an arrogant and unrepentant heart. The Pharisees of Jesus' time were wonderful examples of this condition, but this lives on and is just as destructive today. Most people, while they will not admit it, are convinced that at least in some areas of their life, they do not need God. This pride and attitude is most often hiding, covered from view by its owner, but revealed by God to those who will seek Him and walk with Him.

Read carefully these words of Arthur Wallis from his book, *In the Day of Thy Power.*

> Pride finds expression in the lifting up of self and the justifying of self before God and man. It is the subtle, evasive influence behind many of the works of the flesh. It quickly leads to disobedience to God. When thwarted or humiliated it gives way to envy and bitterness. In order to justify itself it will not hesitate to slander, or speak evil of others. In the pursuit of its ends it may readily stoop to hypocrisy and deceit. Pride is fruitful of all manner of disorders and division amongst the people of God. It is perhaps the greatest enemy of revival, and the most difficult to diagnose and deal with. The most deceitful thing in the world is the heart of man, and only God can truly know it. Pride is woven into the warp and woof of it, and only the Spirit of God can expose it. We dare not search our own hearts, but can only cry out to God like David.
>
> *Search me, O God, and know my heart; try me, and know my anxieties; and see if there is any wicked way in me, and lead me in the way everlasting.*
>
> Psalm 139:23-24 (NKJV)

For thus says the High and Lofty One who inhabits eternity, whose name is Holy: "I dwell in the high and holy place, with him who has a contrite and humble spirit, to revive the spirit of the humble, and to revive the heart of the contrite ones".

ISAIAH 57:15 (NKJV)

And you shall remember that the Lord your God led you all the way these forty years in the wilderness, to humble you and test you, to know what was in your heart, whether you would keep His commandments or not.

DEUTERONOMY 8:2 (NKJV)

There has been a great deal of misapplication of the concept of what it means to humble ourselves. It has been taken to strange and bizarre extremes, missing the mark of God's plan and desire. To be humble is to take our rightful place before God.

Jesus, as always, is our best example. He was a humble man, as He walked the earth; His humbleness was manifest in how He walked as God's Son. The power of the Holy Spirit flowed through Him as He walked out the direction and desires of God the Father. He walked in the anointing of God, fully in tune with God's will and ways. He knew who He was and the power of that position.

The humble person walks in the fullness of the anointing of God. He makes no boast of self, but does not limit, lessen, or lie about the power, and position of a child of God. The humble person walks, dead to self and alive to God. He walks with God and for God. This is a place where the power and abilities of God flow through God's man or woman. To the world the humble man may seem bold and brash, but it is the outworking of the anointing flowing unhindered by self and self aggrandizement. This is how the power of God flowed through Jesus and it is how it is designed to flow through us.

> *Therefore humble yourselves under the mighty hand of*
> *God, that He may exalt you in due time,*
>
> 1 PETER 5:6 (NKJV)

> *Humble yourselves in the sight of the Lord, and He will*
> *lift you up.*
>
> JAMES 4:10 (NKJV)

To be effective in prayer we must have the anointing of the Holy Spirit. When Samuel anointed David, he was guided to David by God's search of the heart. The Holy Spirit comes today to anoint, guided by the God's search of our hearts.

Let us pray!

Articles 13

LIKE EAGLES

O ver the years I have had a bad habit. I have had it as long as I can remember. I tend to interrupting people when they talk jumping into the middle of their sentence. I have even been known to finish sentences for people or answer questions, before they are asked. It is a rude and nasty habit.

I once got a job as a computer operator for a company that processed the production of oil wells. We calculated the royalty checks for people and businesses from the monthly oil production. Some of the checks were just a few dollars, but others were hundreds of thousands of dollars and they got a check like this every month! When I was hired for this job, they planned to give me 6 to 8 weeks of training, but they had a man quit and they needed someone on the swing shift (from 4 to 12 pm). So they asked me to change to swing shift. They said we would complete my training there.

The first afternoon on swing shift, when I walked in the office I could tell that something was amiss. One of our computer programs had failed and the royalty checks for our best client were wrong. What a mess to walk into. I assumed that I would just watch and learn as they discussed what to do. Finally they got the computer program corrected and it was now time to test it and then run it.

This is when my habit began to rise up. I tried to stay out of the way, but soon I was at the computer console of one of those massive computers, the ones that filled an entire room. I started telling people what to do. "Go get that disk pack and mount it over there." "Put the blank tape on that drive and the old tape on this drive." "Go get ready to load the check stock paper in the printer."

Suddenly I realized that even though I was the new man, I was telling my boss what to do, and his boss, and his boss. When I realized what I had done, it was too late to get my words back. Great, first day and I have really messed up bad, I thought. Then I saw that all of them, all my bosses, were doing just what I told them to do. The program worked and we got the job done. Later that night my supervisor and I had a laugh over the incident, but he suggested that it might not be wise to make a practice of telling my bosses what to do.

> *He gives power to the weak, and to those who have no might He increases strength. Even the youths shall faint and be weary, and the young men shall utterly fall, but those who wait on the Lord shall renew their strength; they shall mount up with wings like eagles, they shall run and not be weary, they shall walk and not faint.*
>
> ISAIAH 40:29-31 (NKJV)

Everyone loves this famous passage from Isaiah. And what is there not to like, to be renewed and strengthen, to run and not be weary, to walk and not faint, this is wonderful, a blessing from God. To live in the world, especially at this time, is to face the prospect of growing weary and to be weak, to fail and have no strength. It is easy to faint, so this passage is a timely blessing.

People have also stumbled over this passage as well. As is true in so many of God's promises, this promise comes with a condition. They that wait receive the promise. The problem is "waiting" on or for the Lord.

We live in a time that hates to wait. We have thousands of devices and tools designed to keep us from having to wait. We will go to great lengths and pay a lot of money, to keep from waiting. This is true in the spiritual world as well, we hate to wait. Spiritually this refusal to wait, causes us to be weak, and hinders our prayers.

Lost in the rush of modern Christianity is much of what makes the Christian strong. We rush into church, worship, Bible study, and life and then we dash off to something else. This is ruinous to a strong and victorious Christian life and especially devastating to effective prayer. We lament the loss of power, but we will not wait for God.

Waiting on God in prayer is very important and has become a lost art. We have attempted to put God and prayer in the fast mode of life, expecting instant prayers and answers. We rush in and tell God what we want and how He is to do things. Many of the "How to pray" teachings (and I must admit I have aided in some ways in this), teach us to do "this and that" and then with expectations high, we dash boldly into the throne room of God. We command Him and expect Him to answer quickly, as we want, and then to allow us to dash on with the important things of life. How often we are like I was that day in the computer room, telling my bosses what to do?

> *Oh, the depth of the riches both of the wisdom and knowledge of God! How unsearchable are His judgments and His ways past finding out! "For who has known the mind of the Lord? Or who has become His counselor?" "Or who has first given to Him and it shall be repaid to him?" For of Him and through Him and to Him are all things, to whom be glory forever. Amen.*
>
> ROMANS 11:33-36 (NKJV)

There are many applications to waiting on the Lord. And if we are going to have power in prayer, if we are going to have effective prayer, we must learn these lessons. There is a walk with the Lord, a walk that moves at the Lords beck and call. It proceeds as He directs. In this walk there is power and might. In this walk there is intercession that moves people and nations. It brings mighty changes to the outcome of wars and revolutions. The walk begins with waiting.

Look at just one example of how the mad rush of today has affected our prayer time. Everyone knows the importance of the Word of God in our prayers. We gain faith by the Word, we are guided by the Word, and we are corrected by the Word. There is great value and power in praying the Word of God. His Word is to be our proclamation and confession. There is nothing as powerful or as comforting as the Word of God. And yet, how easy it is to put the Word of God in the fast mode of our days and rush about with it. Instead of walking with Him, we throw the Word into our prayers and then continue on our dash about.

The study of the life and habits of men and women, who have been mighty in prayer, reveal many insights helpful for our training in prayer. One of the habits, often seen, is praying through the Bible. We read of this habit and see the practice of daily reading, passage by passage, through the Bible. This is not just reading, but a central part of their prayers. In this practice they allow God to speak and direct the time of prayer. This is a very powerful form of waiting.

Each day, time would be spent with God, and each day, the Holy Spirit would highlight His message, teaching, or command. It was not driven by the man or woman or circumstance; they could not bring their favorite passage or the verses they felt served the need of the day. They yielded to the Holy Spirit and waited. Often the wait time yielded dealings with the individual who was praying; and how many of us need this type of dealing, making right our heart, renewing our soul, and empowering our obedience.

Like Moses when he spent time with God, and when he came out his face shown bright, so we can be changed if we spend time with God. Often the testimony of friends was that when these men and women of prayer came from this time of waiting in the Word, with God, they had a holy glow and radiance. They also came out of the prayer closet on fire and empowered for the day. Their prayers were powerful and effective. How different are our prayers? We present a few verses of our choosing, and then dash off to stumble through another day.

Some may say they do not have time for something like this. Perhaps, but we can make a start. We can begin by spending time with God. This is not a race to see how much we can read, but to dive deeper and deeper into the depths of the heart of the Father. Spend time with Him is required for powerful prayers. Commit to a time, let the Holy Spirit pick the place in the Word to start, and then take as many days as He wants and do as much as He wants, even just one passage. What is wrong with that, if what we really want is to learn all the Holy Spirit has for us for today?

> *Therefore be patient, brethren, until the coming of the Lord. See how the farmer waits for the precious fruit of the earth, waiting patiently for it until it receives the early and latter rain. You also be patient. Establish your hearts, for the coming of the Lord is at hand.*
>
> JAMES 5:7-8 (NKJV)

It is not enough to talk a good talk, but fail to see the life altering, situation changing, power of God in our prayers. It is not enough for us to have the trickle of answer that is so evident today. The power is still there, the missing ingredient is the man or woman of prayer. God is looking for a person who will join with Him in prayer. He is looking for a person desperate for the power of God; so desperate they are willing to be changed by God.

The question is what do we want? To continue as we are, yields the results we have received. However, there is much more. We can have power in prayer, we can be the man or the woman that God uses for great things in prayer, if we will allow Him to mold us and make us. God is not a respecter of persons, what He has done for and with others He can and will do for and with us.

Effective prayer begins with the prayer, "God change me". There can be a wonderful depth of relationship with God; most people have scarcely scratched the surface. We have often ignored His invitation to come and spend time with Him. To be, powerful in prayer, effective in ministry, and to fulfill all God has designed for us to do, we need to go further and deeper in with God. Will we wait with Him?

For too long and in far too many places, prayer as been more like the foolishness of that new computer operator telling his bosses what to do. Now we need wise people who wait on God, who learn from Him, who are changed by Him, and who are empower by Him. We need people who will wait on the Lord and become willing to do whatever it takes to walk with Him and be powerful in prayer.

Let us pray!

Article 14

PARTNERS

The style and beauty of their movements made them the best. Fred Astaire and Ginger Rogers were for many years, recognized by one and all as the great partnership of the dance floor. At a time when dance had beauty and flowed across the floor, with a flare of elegance, when great dancers were held in high esteem, Fred and Ginger were unsurpassed. Even today shows like "Dancing with the Stars" present a variety of dance partners and if the dance partners are very good they are compared to the standard of Fred and Ginger. Fred Astaire was recognized as the best dancer of all time, although many say Ginger Rogers must have that distinction, after all, she did everything he did and she did it backwards and in high heels!

There have been great partnerships since the beginning of time. When I was a little boy one of the great partnerships was responsible for the Greatest Show on Earth. And as a boy of five I thought they had a great claim to the title. This was self proclaimed title for the circus of Ringling Brothers, Barnum and Bailey. This partnership was the result of a merger of the great circuses of America in the early 1900s. I still remember the night my aunt and uncle took me to the circus in Denver. The sounds, smells, lights, the feats of daring, the animals, performers, and the food, all created wonderful memories of The Greatest Show on Earth.

The Bible also has many great partnerships walking out God's plan and will: David and Jonathan, Moses and Aaron, Peter, James, and John, and Paul and Timothy, to name a few. In more recent times there have been many famous partnerships for the Gospel: John and Charles Wesley, William Wilberforce and William Pitt the Younger, William and Catherine Booth, D.L Moody and Ira Sankey, Billy Graham and George Beverly Shea, and many others.

The greatest partnership of all times, bar none, is that of God the Father and Jesus Christ. Jesus described this partnership, He simply said, "*I and My Father are one*". That is a tight knit partnership and one of great power.

This partnership created the universe and brought salvation to fallen man. This partnership delivers the bound, heals the sick, frees the captive, provides for the poor, loves the unloved, and comforts those who mourn. And while men and women have enjoyed the benefits of many partnerships down through history, there have never been so many, so deeply touched, as by the great work of this, what is the greatest partnership.

This partnership had and continues to have great success. One part of their achievement is from prayer; Jesus was and is a Man of prayer and in His partnership with the Father we see the power and effectiveness of prayer. It reveals all that prayer can be and should be. Jesus' power in prayer is available to all Christians who will follow His example and be guided and taught by the Holy Spirit. The keystone to His success in prayer was his partnership with the Father. The same success can be ours as well.

The Father would like to form a partnership in prayer with each of us. Our salvation opens the door of opportunity to join the partnership. From there God's desire is to build a partnership in prayer. A partnership, by definition, is one party associated with another in an action, sharing a common interest or participating in achieving a common goal. This is what we need and is what we should desire in prayer, a partnership with the Father.

Now some people may object to this idea. They say to claim a partnership with God is elevating your self to a high position and demeaning God. However, Christianity is all about partnership with God. In Christ we become one with Jesus and one with the Father. Partnership in prayer is the action part of God's plan. This is what Jesus wants and what He has been seeking for us. The problem is finding someone willing to be a partner.

> *Now I am no longer in the world, but these are in the world, and I come to You. Holy Father, keep through Your name those whom You have given Me, that they may be one as We are.*
>
> JOHN 17:11 (NKJV)

> *that they all may be one, as You, Father, are in Me, and I in You; that they also may be one in Us, that the world may believe that You sent Me.*
>
> JOHN 17:21 (NKJV)

Where there is a willing man or woman, God initiates a partnership of prayer. God pours in His love and concerns, His desires and longings, causing His heart attitudes and plans to wells up in the heart of the man or woman of the partnership. In His partner, this God-given impartation, swells until it is given voice; God's partner now speaks, in faith and love, the prayer. God hears and responds with His power and in His love, justice, and mercy. From this partnership with God come incredible prayers and answers.

So what do we do to be willing partners with God? First, and foremost, we must walk with God. The partnership of Abraham and God is a good guide for us here. Abraham and God were friends. Abraham believed his friend God, so when it came to prayer the partners talked and Abraham prayed.

> And the Scripture was fulfilled which says, "Abraham believed God, and it was accounted to him for righteousness." And he was called the friend of God.
> JAMES 2:23 (NKJV)

> And the Lord said, "Shall I hide from Abraham what I am doing,"
> GENESIS 18:17 (NKJV)

> Then the men turned away from there and went toward Sodom, but Abraham still stood before the Lord. And Abraham came near and said, "Would You also destroy the righteous with the wicked? Suppose there were fifty righteous within the city; would You also destroy the place and not spare it for the fifty righteous that were in it?"
> GENESIS 18:22-24 (NKJV)

Partners do what they see and hear from the Father. This is what Jesus did in His partnership. Can we do anything different and be successful? Our prayers should be what we hear our Father say and what He wants. This includes God's initiation of our prayers, belief in His faithfulness, and seeking His will over our own.

> I can of Myself do nothing. As I hear, I judge; and My judgment is righteous, because I do not seek My own will but the will of the Father who sent Me.
> JOHN 5:30 (NKJV)

Partners seek to have a soft heart before God. They work to keep all hindrance from their heart, so they can hear Him. The hindrance of things like iniquity is a barrier that blocks hearing from God and God hearing from us.

If I regard iniquity in my heart, The Lord will not hear.
PSALM 66:18 (NKJV)

Partners have faith. They know that God is faithful to His promises and plans. They have faith that moves mountains because their faith comes from knowing God's will and His faithful nature. The faith-filled man or woman walks in the faithfulness of God.

By faith Sarah herself also received strength to conceive seed, and she bore a child when she was past the age, because she judged Him faithful who had promised.
HEBREWS 11:11 (NKJV)

Today is a time of great difficulties and challenges with many problems and needs. The answer to the needs of today and in the future, is the prayer partnership. The partnership of a man or woman of prayer with God yields the answers we so desperately need. God is looking for partners; will you be a prayer partner with God?

Let us pray!

Article 15

3 DAYS BEFORE ANSWERS

My Grandma had a gift store and one of the most popular items she sold were her cookbooks. She wrote and my aunt illustrated these simple books. One of the best was her *3 Days before Payday* cookbook. The premise of this cookbook was that it was possible to fix good meals for your family even when you got down to that time, a few days before the next payday, when the cupboard and the refrigerator were low on supplies. This cookbook was more than just recipes, it offered complete meal plans. With these plans you could creatively provide a good and nutritious meal for your family.

One of the facts of life is that we all face trials. There are difficulties that must be overcome if we are going to be successful in life; this is true in general and especially true in our Christian life. When Christians are actively involved in Church life and activities like the sharing of their faith or effective prayer, they must deal with the trials and hindrances. Trials are a part of life.

We may wish this was not so, but it is so, and to be successful we have to deal with trials. Our time on earth is not just to be endured, but is a time for us to be conquerors. Jesus came to earth, lived, died, and rose from the dead, for us, so we can have an abundant life. This life is ours by the grace of God, but there are forces that strive to keep us from living this life. Between the work of the Devil, the lust of our flesh, and the lure of the world, we face many trials. And overcoming these trials is important, it is part of our preparation to live and reign as the glorious Bride of Christ. This Bride is learning how to deal with every force hostile to God and His Kingdom.

Prayer, described in simple terms, is conquering over trials and hindrances. What do we do when we face a trial? Are we overcome and forced to suffer loss or do we rise up and conquer? The man or woman successful in prayer does the later. Most of us are still learning the lessons of conquering. We pray, but too often our prayers are weak, ineffective prayers that avail little, if anything. We see the possibilities and we long to triumph, but we struggle.

One of the most difficult times in our efforts to be successful, in prayer, is when we face time between our prayer and the manifestation of the answer. The Devil, the lust of our flesh, and the lure of the world, often attack during this period. For success in prayer we must continue in faith until we have the answer in hand. We must not turn from God and His promises. We must not respond to the clamor of doubt, fear, and unbelief.

By making a slight change to the title of the little cookbook my Grandma wrote, it becomes a description of what we face. In her book the difficulty was feeding her family those last few days before the next payday. Our difficulty is dealing with the trials of waiting for the answer to our prayers to be manifest. Grandma in her book suggested ways to have meals from things found at home and with little money. We find ways to continue in faith through the trial until victory of the answer coming. So today I present for our benefit, *3 Days before Answers*.

What can we, should we, must we do, to go through the trial until we receive the answer to our prayer? This is a massive subject and more suited to treatment in a book rather than just an article, but there are some basics that we should know and things we can do.

The underlining key is to keep the faith. If our faith fails, so have we. In his letter to the Ephesians, Paul says, having done all, then, stand. And what he is talking about is to stand in faith. All of the other things we address in this study, or any other on the subject of effective prayer, are wasted, if we quit. Even if it seems as though the game is over, do not quit. We are children of the Almighty God and things are not over until God says they are over. This also means that faith is working until we get our answer, as long as we do not quit.

Stand therefore, having girded your waist with truth,
having put on the breastplate of righteousness,

EPHESIANS 6:14 (NKJV)

What do we do to stand in faith? What can we, should we, must we do, to maintain our faith when the pressure is on? A very important ingredient in our recipe for conquering in trials is thanksgiving. Thanksgiving is so important; it changes the conditions we face, it is like turning on God's light in our life.

When you walk in a room at night, the first thing you do is turn on the light; it is so automatic we do not even think about it. Thanksgiving should be the first thing, the things we automatically reach for, when we pray. This is especially true when we are dealing with delays in receiving answers. The longer the wait, the more we need thanksgiving.

When we face problems and we have needs, we want answers and sometime we are desperate for answers. If the answers we seek come quickly, then we are happy and rejoice in the blessing of God. If the answers are slow to come, then things are more of a struggle and there is a danger of becoming angry with God. The anger of man is not the foundation for faith, but it can destroy our faith. Slipping into (or leaping into) anger is one of the reasons why so many people do not pray effective prayers that avail much.

However, when we walk, day-by-day, declaring our thanksgiving to God, we can overcome anger. With thanksgiving, we can clear away the darkness of despair and frustration. With thanksgiving, we declare the goodness of God and all His blessings. We thank Him for the wonderful things He has done and for the things He will do.

> *Enter into His gates with thanksgiving, And into His courts with praise. Be thankful to Him, and bless His name.*
>
> PSALM 100:4 (NKJV)

> *Be anxious for nothing, but in everything by prayer and supplication, with thanksgiving, let your requests be made known to God;*
>
> PHILIPPIANS 4:6 (NKJV)

> *Continue earnestly in prayer, being vigilant in it with thanksgiving;*
>
> COLOSSIANS 4:2 (NKJV)

In the prayer cupboard there are many other wonderful ingredients, provided by God, described in the Bible, and empowered by faith. These ingredients are for our use, things like, love, forgiveness, perseverance, standing on His promises, abiding in Christ, and the list goes on and on. These are just a few of the provisions God has made for us. If we successfully deal with the challenges of *3 Days before Answers*, then we can have great victory in prayer.

Men and women of victorious prayer conquer by . . .

3 DAYS BEFORE ANSWERS

Stop! Instead of just reading this article, you finish writing it. Write out your recipe for dealing with the *3 Days before Answers*. Write a personal recipe for dealing with the trials of waiting for the answer. What are the things you do and things you should be doing, to stay in faith until the answer comes. Be specific and practical. Remember in my Grandma's cookbook there were not just recipes, but complete meal plans. Write your recipe for a complete meal, all you need to do, say, and think, to have success throughout the day and each day until the answer comes. Write out the things you can and will do, to be victorious.

Let us pray!

Article 16

FACING THE GRANITE WALL

I n the 1860s a couple of companies set out to build a railroad that
would run from coast to coast across the American continent.
This was a huge undertaking, challenging the abilities, resources, and
determination of these men. There was great fame and wealth for the
group that first accomplished this goal, but there were great difficulties
that they would have to overcome to succeed.

The Union Pacific Railroad began in the middle of the continent near
Omaha, Nebraska and built to the west. The Central Pacific Railroad
began on the West Coast and built to the east. Between them was the
Sierra Nevada Mountains; a range of mountains so steep and difficult
that most people assumed no railroad could traverse this obstacle.

Lead by Charles Crocker of the Central Pacific Railroad, a force of up
to 12,000 workers push from the coast into the mountains of California.
Rising up before them were almost insurmountable difficulties. The rails
had to go across swift rivers, over deep canyons, and cling to narrow
ledges that were hacked into sheer walls and hung over high precipices.
In some places there was just no place for the rails and they had to go
through the mountains, via long tunnels. In other places the roadbed and

tracks had to be covered by massive snow sheds, to stop the destruction of massive avalanches, far too common in the harsh winters. Their effort was made even tougher due to the type of rock in these mountains. The ledges and tunnels had to be cut through some of the toughest granite found anywhere in the world.

Finally, in 1869, the Central Pacific Railroad was able to successfully traverse the Sierra Nevada Mountains. They then rushed across Nevada. In a big ceremony, with President Grant in attendance, they met with the Union Pacific Railroad at Promontory Point in Utah. These companies had conquered the seemingly impossible.

Many of you who are reading this are facing difficult tasks. The difficulties rise up before you like the granite of the Sierra Nevada Mountains. Many of you have been praying and working to deal with thorny and complex situations for many years.

You know what the railroad builders faced when people laughed and ridicule these men and when they called them dreamers or just plain crazy. And even while they were building the railroad there were hindrances that would have been too much for most people; workers quit (that is why they finally had to use Chinese immigrants as workers), the weather was too difficult, the snow was too deep, the grades were too steep, there was not enough money, there were lawsuits, and the list goes on and on. However, they continued working and finally were successful.

You also face difficulties in completing those things God has given you to accomplish. In work and prayer you face insurmountable situations and obstacles. You also hear from people who tell you that you will not be successful. In many ways it seems you are trying to do and are asking for, the impossible. The author of Isaiah knew what you are going through and described this type of situation.

> *And He said to me, 'You are My servant, O Israel, in whom I will be glorified.' Then I said, 'I have labored*

in vain, I have spent my strength for nothing and in vain: . . .

ISAIAH 49:3-4 (NKJV)

Isaiah was called by God, His servant. You have been called as God's servant. Isaiah faced difficult, seemingly impossible situations. You face the difficult and seemingly impossible. Isaiah knew that he would rest in the glory of God. And you know that Heaven's gate is waiting for you. And then Isaiah pours out the hurt in his heart saying, "I have labored in vain, I have worked until I have no strength left and I have nothing to show for all my work" (author's paraphrase). If you have prayed for long working hard and prayed hard for things deemed impossible, you have faced great difficulties. And you can relate to Isaiah's lament.

There were many times when it seemed the builders of the Central Pacific Railroad were not making any progress at all. For example, in some places the black power used as the explosive of the day, did nothing except make a black mark on the surface of the granite. In desperation Crocker brought in nitroglycerin, which at that time was a new and powerful explosive, but it was also unstable and very dangerous to use. It was so unstable that there was no safe way to transport it, so they had to mix it near the worksite; a practice that often yielded deadly and destructive, unexpected explosions.

Even with nitroglycerin the progress was slow. At one stage in the process, his crews spent several months just building one tunnel. Crocker had teams of workers working around the clock and they were working from both ends of the tunnel, but for several months not even one section of track was laid. To the world it seemed as though they were making no progress at all. The naysayers had a field day; surely this was proof that this railroad could not be built.

The builders of the railroad could have given up on their battle, but they did not. We can give up on our prayer battles, or press on to completion of the assignment and success. The railroad builders could also have been stubborn and continued to try to cut through the granite with black power. This was the explosive everyone used and the safe thing to do. If they had done this, they would still be cutting tunnels.

Opposition stands before everyone who prays. We can listen to the naysayers and quit or we can continue to press on, trusting in God's direction, power, and His final assessment of our work. Secondly, we can run the danger of being stubborn in what we do and how we pray, not correcting any errors in our ways. If we do this then we will never receive the answers we seek and need.

Men and women of prayer face times of difficulty. They are praying and praying and praying, but sometimes it seems as though nothing is happening. It can be very frustrating and everyone can see that there is no progress is being made toward the answer. It is easy to lament as Isaiah did, however, read what follows his lament.

> *Yet surely my just reward is with the Lord, and my work with my God*
>
> ISAIAH 49:4 (NKJV)

The word translated as "reward" in the NKJV is "judgment" in the KJV. In the Hebrew this word means a verdict. What God is reminding Isaiah, and through him reminding us, the final word on progress, success, and value of our prayer and work, rests with God. He never judges these things with incomplete knowledge. God knows the end result and His verdict is based on sound judgment, not half truths or partial information.

If we judge the worth and progress of our prayers we run the risk of error because we do not know all the facts. If we allow the world, the media, or others to judge our worth and progress, we can be confident that their judgment is inaccurate. We have been called to prayer. We are God's vessel, called for His purpose and plan; here to pray and receive His answers.

If we are going to pray through the granite wall that is in front of us, then we must properly deal with the difficulties that face effective prayer. We must not allow premature, erroneous, misinformed, improper, incomplete, judgments, to hinder or stop our work of prayer. We must trust God to direct us and help us, and leave the judgment of worth and success to Him. We also must submit to inspection and guidance by the Holy Spirit of our prayers, our character, our work, and our faith. Then we must have a willingness to make the changes as He directs as well as how and when He directs. We must remember that God is working in us and with us to bring His answers to the seemingly impossible situations we face.

Let us pray!

Article 17

RAZOR SHARP

When I was a teenager I worked several summers for my grandparents. They ran a gift shop and mail order business. We would send out orders to people all over America and around the world. One very popular item was a round terrycloth hand towel to be hung on the front of a kitchen cabinet.

My grandfather and I would cut stacks of terrycloth for workers who would sew on rickrack border and a bow to complete the towel. My grandfather made an adjustment to a power jigsaw so we could attach a cut-throat razor blade and cut fifty layers of terrycloth in one pass. To use a razor blade it had to be very sharp and you would sharpen it using a leather strop. This is where I first saw and practiced sharpening with a strop to make a blade razor sharp.

For centuries men have been getting up every morning and shaving their face whiskers. For years they used a straight razor, sometimes called an open razor or cut-throat razor. A man would get up and splash some soap and water on his face and strop the blade to make it as sharp as possible. Once the stropping was completed, the man could get a close, safe, and comfortable shave.

Power in prayer comes to those who seek God with their whole heart; for those who are razor sharp. Unfortunately, many Christians live their life as though, "good as most, better than some" was okay. If we lived in a Christian society where the general standard was very high, this attitude might not be too bad. But, we don't. To be as "good as most", even "better than some" leaves much room for iniquity and decadence. And if we are going to have power in prayer, we must learn to live at a much higher standard.

Oswald Chamber with the title of his famous book sums up the need we have today. The title is *My Utmost, for His Highest*. We need men and women striving to give our utmost for His highest. We need to seek to be our best, even in our frailty and failings, so we can pray with power and have wonderful answers to our prayers.

We can live like the world, and have weak, anemic prayers, if we pray at all. Or we can allow God to strop us so we are razor sharp. God wants us to be perfect without nick or blemish, ready for powerful, effective prayer. He is calling for a holy people, fully committed to Him and seeking to be razor sharp for victorious prayer.

> *that He might present her to Himself a glorious church,*
> *not having spot or wrinkle or any such thing, but that*
> *she should be holy and without blemish.*
> EPHESIANS 5:27 (NKJV)

There are many things we need to do to be razor sharp for prayer. One is to cultivate the skills and lifestyle we need. Preparation is a key to success in many fields, but it is often hard work, with long hours of study and practice requiring a dedication to strive for mastery. The great people in any field are those who work hard, paying the price of preparation, and then their efforts pay off. Cultivation is defined as, to prepare for use, to foster growth, to improve by labor, care, or study, or to refine things such as the mind.

Everyone cultivates areas in their life. The key is to be wise in our cultivation. Unfortunately, for many people the focus is on the negative things in life. The cultivation of worldly things causes worry, pain, suffering, fear, doubt, and destruction. Cultivation of the world into our life is easy. Daily there is a, nearly non-stop, flow of information and data that is not godly, nor is it edifying. And while most people view inputs from the world as innocuous, it is deceptive, dangerous, and can be deadly.

Cultivation in a Christian context is doing everything we can so we can walk with the Lord. This is removing everything in our life, communication, and thoughts that would separate us from God's presence. Christian cultivation is walking day-by-day with the Holy Spirit as our close companion. We make Him our Holy Guest and walk, talk, and act as we would do when we are in the presence of a special or honored person.

Cultivation is giving God first place in our life. This is putting the Word of God in our heart. And more than just some Word there, it is putting the Word in our heart in abundance. It is out of the abundance of our heart that the mouth speaks. Right speaking in general, and even more importantly, right speaking in prayer, is cultivated by filling our heart to full and overflowing with the Word of God.

Cultivating a victorious Christian life is dealing with unbelief, doubt, fear, unforgiveness, pride, hardness of heart, and jealousy. Cultivating is developing, nurturing, fostering, promoting, encouraging, supporting, and helping live the life God has planned for us.

Abraham cultivated razor sharp prayer by cultivating faith and obedience. It is natural that we should learn razor sharp prayer from Abraham, a man of great faith and prayer. Abraham walked in faith not being moved by what he saw. Even though his body seem old and as good as dead concerning having a child, Abraham believed God and declared what God said to be true over what he saw.

And he walked in obedience to God. When he made covenant with God, Abraham drove away the vultures; which represent everything that would steal his faith. When God told him to take his son Isaac and give him as an offering to God, he went immediately. As a bonus, please note he did not say anything bad, he was convinced that God would even resurrect his son, if need be.

We could look at many other examples of the men and women of the Bible cultivating a life that made them razor sharp for prayer. And are you one of these examples, cultivated to a razor sharp point, ready to pray effective fervent prayers that avail much?

Let us pray!

Article 18

THE BEST

B eing stationed in Germany was one of the best things that ever happened to me. For three years I was in Germany as part of my enlistment in the United States Air Force and I lived on a small Air Station in Wiesbaden, Germany and worked in a smaller base nearby. I got to travel and learn about Germany and much of Western Europe. For a young man from Colorado, who had never even thought much of travel, this was a great opportunity and adventure. There were many interesting and wonderful things that I experienced; one of the most exciting was the 1974 World Cup.

The World Cup is the championship of soccer. This competition pits the best teams from nations around the world. This was a very exciting time in Germany, as the German team was very good and Germany was the host nation. Germany had not won the World Cup since 1954 so the loyal supporters of Germany, where "football" (soccer) is very popular, yearned for another title. All spring the build up to the tournament was amazing. Everywhere you went in Germany people were talking about the team. It was on the news daily and many of the preliminary games were televised. This was very unusual for a time before a plethora of channels and multiple "all sport" networks on TV.

Germany did well and kept advancing. Finally the day of the finals arrived. The dream that seemed nearly impossible a few months ago was now only one win away. Germany nearly came to a standstill during the time of the match. People watched on TV and also gathered in the central square of towns across Germany to listen to reports of the game. Finally it happened, Germany beat the Netherlands 2-1 and Germany was the World Champion!

The celebration was greater than anything I had ever experienced. People gathered in cities and towns, they sang and shouted until the early hours of the morning. And they set off fireworks; the massive explosions filled the skies over Wiesbaden for nearly an hour. It was finally official, Germany was the best!

The best means, excelling over all others, it is to be the most productive of good or of advantage, utility, or satisfaction. To "excel" or to be the "most productive of good" has a very good sound to it. Many times people have thrilled to the sound of those words when they are given in reference to their team or activities.

And as Christians we know about the best. In everything that is good, honorable, and proper, Jesus lived His life on earth, as the best. When a person is looking for the standard of how things should be done, Jesus is the bench mark of perfection. He is the high standard of God concerning man; He is the Best of the best.

When Jesus lived on earth, He lived as a man. Everything He did was as a man, with the same abilities and capabilities that all men and women possess. He used the power of the Holy Spirit to do the miraculous things He did, just as we can. He trusted the Holy Spirit to lead and guide Him through daily life and many trials, just as we can. His provisions, miracles, and ministry was empowered by and directed by the Holy Spirit, just as it can be for us today. He shows how all men should live. To be the best today is to live as Jesus lived.

Striving to be the best is the way that man was made. God's design includes a desire and the drive to be fruitful, subdue the earth, and have dominion. In a word, that is a call to be the best. Regardless of our station or location, God is calling us to be like Jesus. He is calling us to be the best. If you are a son or a mother, a worker or an employer, a student or retired, a daughter or father, a minister or inventor, in any and all walks of life, we should be seeking to be the best.

And to be the best, Jesus is the standard we must seek to emulate. By His standard the best is defined as full of faith, high in character, self-sacrificing, hard working, always motivated by love, and powerful in prayer. When we are like Jesus, regardless of where we are or what we are doing, we are the best.

What is the best in prayer? The best in prayer, seeks to live and pray like Jesus. The best always prays in faith, always prays seeking God's will, always prays for the Kingdom to come here on earth as it is in Heaven, and always prays in love. The best always prays, knowing that God hears and when He hears, He answers. The best always expects the supernatural to happen, knowing that it is God's nature. The best always prays, ready and available to obey the Holy Spirit and pray and do as He directs.

> *Most assuredly, I say to you, he who believes in Me, the works that I do he will do also; and greater works than these he will do, because I go to My Father. And whatever you ask in My name, that I will do, that the Father may be glorified in the Son. If you ask anything in My name, I will do it.*
>
> JOHN 14:12-14 (NKJV)

These articles are written to challenge you to be the best; the best in prayer. In all you do, both in prayer and every other endeavor, seek the high standard. Seek to be like Jesus, our great and glorious standard. Seek to be the best!

Let us pray!

TIME FOR PRAYER

I n college I was a history major and with this background I often look at things with a historian's eye or view point. That does not mean that all historians think alike or even agree on things, we most certainly do not. It does mean that my training is such that I look at people and events as part of a sweep of history. I tend to look for patterns; for long term trends, and for the role men and women have had in shaping events.

If we looked at revivals as an example, we can look for patterns and trends. Study of revivals in America shows an interesting pattern of having a revival about every fifty years. The pattern is not followed all over the world. There are places that have had several revivals, but not on a regular cycle. There are places that have not yet had a revival. Most revivals feature a powerful move of God, a repentance of sins, and a powerful evangelistic drive (often both locally and in missions). And the most notable feature of revivals is that they come by an outpouring of prayer.

From my point of view, we need a major revival today. This is true in America and many other parts of the world. Please note, when I talk of revival I am not speaking of renewal. In many place we have renewals in various churches, this is good and needed, but this is a move of God in a church and with mostly Christians.

Revival, as I use the word, is a move of God that changes Christians and the society of the region. In the Welsh Revival of 1904, once the revival began, there were virtually no crimes reported for weeks, the taverns were importing less than a ten percent of the pre-revival, barrels of drink, policemen had nothing to do except crowd control and singing in quartets that performed at special events. The Welsh society was changed. That is the kind of change we need now. And this revival, and the others it spawned around the world, began by an outpouring of prayer.

In the last days of the Roman Republic; Julius Caesar, after conquering the region of Gaul (what is today France) marched his army toward Rome. He came to the Rubicon River and a point of decision. With him was a massive army; one of the most powerful forces anywhere at that time, and they were loyal to him, not to Rome. The government of the Roman Republic told him not to come any closer to Rome; he was to stay on the other side of the Rubicon. They knew if he came with his army, he could take over Rome and bring down the republic.

Caesar faced a point of decision, follow the orders or cross over and be the leader of Rome. As all of you, who know history, are aware, he did cross the Rubicon River. He easily took control of the Government and ruled until his death. From his actions and those of his followers, most notably Augustus Caesar, the Roman Republic fell and became an Empire, with a dictator at its head.

My point in reminding you of this event from 2000 years ago is to direct our thoughts to the concept of "point of decision". Today around the world people are facing important points of decision. Some of these are personal and others are on a larger scale. But, just like in the case of Caesar and Rome, for all involved, after this point of decision, things will never be the same.

For some people this is personal point of decision, they stand at their personal Rubicon River. Today is the day of their decision on Christ. We know that in some places there is a powerful move of God at hand and people are making good choices. In other places, people are restricted from hearing the preaching of the Gospel. And without the Good News is very difficult for anyone to make good decisions.

In some places the point of decision is national concerns. In some countries it is time for elections. Some elections will be spirited, but few if any will lose their life in the political process. In other countries voting could be coupled with a likelihood of death. In some places choices are being made that will dictate how people will conduct their life and how they will live.

I do not write this to scare you; I will leave that to the newspapers. I write because I believe we are at a key time, a decision point. The times we live in are like the days and months before revivals. History of revivals is filled with reports of the difficult times that people faced. Many reports of the situation before revivals stated, "We are with our backs against the wall". The situation had gotten so desperate that the people were forced to pray. They had no other choice.

Today the situation as I see it is, "We are with our backs against the wall." This is true in many parts of the world and in a wide array of situations. And there is something we must do. We must pray.

The day in which we live is desperate for prayer. For those of you new to prayer, the call is to begin to pray. Do the best you know how and learn your lessons on prayer quickly so you can do more. Those of you who have been praying for some time, now is the time to redouble your efforts. You can and must make a difference at this time. For those of you who have even more experience under your belt, now is the time to take on the mantle of prayer. The world is desperate for you to step up to the example and standard of great men and women of prayer of the past. It is time to pray!

The articles of Unit Three—*Time to Pray*, are a call to prayer for people and nations. The effective, fervent prayer of a righteous man avails much. This must be our goal and make it the reality of our prayer life. Our powerful prayers are needed now. Remember that before the great revivals in history, most people believed there was no hope. Then people, just like you and me, began to pray. They became fervent in prayer, they became effective in prayer and they saw God do the seemingly impossible. He will do the same today, if we will pray. Now more than ever, it is time to pray!

Article 19

OPEN DOORS

G eneral Washington finally saw his opportunity. The war had drug on and on, campaign-after-campaign, year-after-year. There had been the dark days of Valley Forge, the desperate days, when survival was all that could be hoped for. Survival was the subject of daily prayers and these prayers had been answered, and the army had survived. Now his prayers were for seeking a way to win the war and winning seemed just as impossible as survival had been earlier.

For years Washington had been looking for a way to strike a decisive blow against the British and win the American Revolution. He was able to win several victories and there were fewer defeats, but he just could not find an opportunity to have the big win, one great win that would lead to final victory.

Now the moment was at hand. Washington had well trained troops available who could travel quickly. They were ready to fight and win against British troops. He also had, for the first time, the possibility of using a large contingent of the French Navy. With the use of the French Navy, Washington could remove a big negative factor, the British Royal Navy. The Royal Navy had always been the X factor, able to overcome any plan of Washington for victory.

Washington quickly walked through this suddenly available open door of opportunity. He sent army troops to pin down the British commander and his army at Yorktown. He sent other troops to complete the encirclement of the area. He had the French Navy to take up a position that forced the British Royal Navy to leave the area. The result; the British commander had to surrender. This was the last great battle of the war. With this win, America broke free from Great Britain and became an independent nation.

An important component of successful prayer is the open door. Much of what happens in life concerns doors; opened or closed. The function of a door is simple; you can go through it if it is open and you cannot pass through if it is closed. We see the concept of the door used in many applications; Jesus lived, died, and He rose from the grave, overcoming death. What He did presents an open door of opportunity for men and women to be saved. Salvation is an open door, inviting all who will, to make a choice, and enter.

Praying for open doors is important factor in successful prayer. We pray about a need and with an open door the answer can come through. Praying for closed doors is equally a part of prayer; an open door can give access to evil as well. So there are times when it is imperative to pray for a door to close. Successful prayer is hearing from God, and then seeking the correct position for the door, open or closed. This applies to praying for individuals, groups, and nations.

This seems so simple, but there can be problems that must be overcome. First we must hear from God. This is fundamental to all prayer. We can throw any request at God, but effective prayer is praying God's will. One of the secrets to Jesus' success in prayer was always praying the will of the Father. Our success comes the same way; when we pray the will of the Father, we are assured of wonderful answers. The problem comes from sin and the noise of the world. These try to keep us separated from God and from hearing His will.

Next, the Bible tells us that faith comes; it comes to those who go and get it. Success in prayer demands faith and the building of a deep faith that God can use. With a constant effort, we can have a steady inflow of the Word of God. With this we can build our faith and have the faith we need for daily living and for effective prayers. Blowing open doors of opportunity and bolting closed doors, requires faith.

Furthermore there are many adversaries that must be overcome. The Devil likes to barricade doors. He knows he is defeated, but he works within the shadows, trying to have his way. He cannot withstand the power of prayer, so he must try to keep people from prayer or at least from effective prayers. He uses many adversaries and these must be removed or overcome. The amour of God is for doing battle and daily we must battle against the shadows and bluster the Devil seeks to bring against us. At times this means we must pray open the doors of our life so we can effectively pray for others.

For a great and effective door has opened to me, and there are many adversaries.

1 CORINTHIANS 16:9 (NKJV)

There are three basic components of an effective open door. To use an open door we must be in the right place, in the right frame of mind, and with the necessary resources. With these three, we can take advantage of the opportunity.

An open door is of no value if we are not in the right place. If we are not where we ought to be, we miss the opportunity. This is not just the physical location, but anything that keep us from being ready and able to walk through the door.

Second, we must be in the right frame of mind. Right frame of mind is how we think and believe. If we are caught up in fear, doubt, anger, unbelief or other sins, if we are not walking in faith and love, if we do not practice the commands of God, we will not be able to step through the opening; we may not even see it.

Third, we must have the resources needed to walk through the door. Without the necessary resources for taking advantage of an open door, the opening is merely a frustration. Resources include many things ranging from money to permissions to abilities. And these come by prayer.

In addition there is something more. I call it, "embrace the race". To pray for and then walk through an open door, we must have a willingness to run the race, and run to win. If we are "just chill'n" on the corner, watching the world go by, then we will missed the opportunity of the open door. For those who will embrace the race, there are battles to be fought and won, accomplishments to be completed, and a life to be lived abundantly. And this is as it should be, life is a race and Christians should run to win.

> *And it happened after this that Ben-Hadad king of Syria gathered all his army, and went up and besieged Samaria.*
>
> 2 KINGS 6:24 (NKJV)

The siege of Samaria by Ben-Haddad brought a great famine. A siege is a blockade of a city and designed to compel it to surrender. Conditions in the city will get bad; people will become frantic for food and water. Finally, when conditions get bad enough, in desperation, people will capitulate. This is what was happening here, the conditions were so bad that the head of a donkey was being sold for about two pounds of silver. In the mist of these terrible conditions, the prophet Elisha boldly declared God's impending deliverance.

> *Then Elisha said, "Hear the word of the Lord. Thus says the Lord: 'Tomorrow about this time a seah of fine*

> *flour shall be sold for a shekel, and two seahs of barley*
> *for a shekel, at the gate of Samaria."*
>
> 2 KINGS 7:1 (NKJV)

The situation seemed impossible; Israel was besieged by the mighty Syrian army and was in the mist of a horrible famine. People were struggling to live and preparing to die. An officer of the king of Israel summed up the situation in response to Elisha's prophecy, "Look, if the Lord would make windows in heaven, could this thing be?"

In the natural, this officer was right. There was no way that the situation could change for the better; no way it could change that much, not in a day. What the officer did not take into account was God. This officer spoke out of unbelief and failed to see that God was able to do the seemingly impossible. Read how Elisha answered this man's unbelief.

> *So an officer on whose hand the king leaned answered*
> *the man of God and said, "Look, if the Lord would*
> *make windows in heaven, could this thing be?" And he*
> *[Elisha] said, "In fact, you shall see it with your eyes,*
> *but you shall not eat of it."*
>
> 2 KINGS 7:2 (NKJV)

You know what happened. God moved against the Syrian army and they fled the battlefield, leaving everything they had. Four men with leprosy discover this fact and alerted the people of Israel, who after a careful check of the story, rush out to gather the supplies left by the Syrians. There was so much plunder that the prices for buying food and the cost supplies, dropped to almost nothing.

> *Then the people went out and plundered the tents of the*
> *Syrians. So a seah of fine flour was sold for a shekel,*

and two seahs of barley for a shekel, according to the word of the Lord.

2 KINGS 7:16 (NKJV)

The rest of the story is that all of Israel was saved from destruction and had plenty, but the officer of the king was trampled by the people rushing out to gather the plunder and he died. He saw God's deliverance, but did not get to eat or enjoy God's provision.

And so it happened to him, for the people trampled him in the gate, and he died.

2 KINGS 7:20 (NKJV)

For Israel, God provided an open door of opportunity. In a situation where it seemed that there was no possibility for a positive outcome, God moved powerfully. When it seemed that nothing could be done to change the situation in a positive way, God opened the doors of Heaven and poured out a blessing. He was not bound by the situation or circumstances, He overcame them.

Praying for and walking through an open door of opportunity requires being in the right place, with the right frame of mind, and with the necessary resources. All of this comes through good training; but too often people's training has come from the world. This training comes from music, news, TV, magazines, radio, books, and conversations. It pours into people's life and often without realizing what is happening, people are trained to think like the world.

The officer of the king of Israel in the story we just read, is a perfect example of this. He had been trained by the world and he knew that changing the situation, like Elisha claimed would happen, was not possible. This officer was a realist; he knew what was possible and more importantly, what was impossible. With this certain knowledge, he was in unbelief concerning the power of God.

Most people today are like this officer. Knowing the reality of the situation, they are in skepticism, doubt, or unbelief concerning the promises of God. This keeps people from going through an open door; often they do not even see a door. The longer people go through life, not seeing the openings of God, the more the training of the world sets their thinking, the more ridged errors in thinking become.

> *whose minds the god of this age has blinded, who do not believe, lest the light of the gospel of the glory of Christ, who is the image of God, should shine on them.*
>
> 2 Corinthians 4:4 (NKJV)

There are things we can do to fight off this rigid, worldly mind set. When we got saved and became a new creation in Christ Jesus; our spirit was born new. We are from that moment a new creation in Christ Jesus. However, our mind, emotions, and will must be transformed. To do so, we must change our old ways of thinking.

> *I beseech you therefore, brethren, by the mercies of God, that you present your bodies a living sacrifice, holy, acceptable to God, which is your reasonable service. And do not be conformed to this world, but be transformed by the renewing of your mind, that you may prove what is that good and acceptable and perfect will of God.*
>
> Romans 12:1-2 (NKJV)

The Word of God is the agent for making a transition from a worldly mind to a right frame of mind. However, even the Bible cannot change us if we do not allow it to work. We must go beyond just reading a few verses and begin to actually train our thinking by immersion in the Word. How many hours each day do you hear and see worldly input? Compare that to the time you are being trained by the Bible. It is no wonder that most people think worldly thoughts and act like the world!

Today, all around us, there are people, ministries, and nations that need open doors of opportunity. God is looking for men and women have been trained by the Word of God and are ready and willing to give of their time to pray for others. In responding to His call to pray, do not forget about praying for the doors. It is time to pray for open doors.

Let us pray!

Article 20

CLOSED DOORS

We had just gotten back from the grocery store. To make it easier to carry the bags of groceries from our car to the house, we propped the storm door open. Just before we closed the door, a house finch made a wrong turn and came into our glassed-in porch. Although the door was still open the finch could not find the opening to make his way out. The windows looked like a good way to escape, but that proved impossible. We were not sure what to do; it was great to sit and watch this finch up close, we did not want to hurt the bird, but we knew it needed to get out. To try to help, we opened the other door. Finally, after many attempts to find an opening through the windows, the finch saw the open door and flew off.

In the previous article we looked at the importance of open doors. However, for the finch that came on our porch, and often for people as well, what is needed is not an open door, but a closed door. If the door had been closed when the finch first came near the porch, then there would not have been those terrifying moments of captivity.

We tend to get excited about open doors and praying for doors to open is a very important part of a successful Christian and effective prayer life. However, there are times when it is more important to have a door closed.

One such time is dealing with the past. All of us have things we have said and done that are not good. We have sown unrighteousness and sin and we have reaped what we have sown. It is important to deal with this aspect of life. The grace of God is available to help us. One aspect of the goodness of God is His willingness to forgive.

If we confess our sins, He is faithful and just to forgive us our sins and to cleanse us from all unrighteousness.
1 JOHN 1:9 (NKJV)

The beauty and value of forgiveness is illustrated by the story of the Prodigal Son. In this story the process of repentance is presented, as well as the great love, mercy, and grace of our Father. In this story we also see one of the values of the closed door, closing the door on our past.

Repentance has two elements. We see these elements in the Hebrew and Greek words that are translated into the English word repentance. The meaning of the Hebrew word for repentance denotes a change of mind. The Prodigal Son "came to himself". This was a change of mind. The meaning for the Greek word for repentance reveals a requirement for a change of direction. When the Prodigal Son started for home he made a change in the direction of his life.

True repentance requires action following our change of mind. It is not enough to just say I am sorry; we must change both our thinking and our actions. We must come to the place where we do not want to think or do the things the way we did them before. We come to a place where we long to be like Jesus and with this new way of thinking, and we act in a new and better way. Our new actions should not be just random acts, but should be in alignment with God's Word, the Bible, and be the actions of an obedient son or daughter, doing the Father's will.

But when he came to himself, he said, 'How many of my father's hired servants have bread enough and to spare, and I perish with hunger! I will arise and go to my father, and will say to him, "Father, I have sinned against heaven and before you, and I am no longer worthy to be called your son. Make me like one of your hired servants." ' And he arose and came to his father. But when he was still a great way off, his father saw him and had compassion, and ran and fell on his neck and kissed him.

LUKE 15:17-20 (NKJV)

The Prodigal Son went back to his father to be a servant, but his father received him back as his son. Our Heavenly Father, like the father in the story, is out looking for us, every day, and is delighted to receive us back when we have sinned. This is wonderful and far better than the best the world has to offer with its therapy sessions and step programs.

There is more to this. To be successful we need to close the door. When we have repented, in both our thinking and action, we then need to close the door on the past. It would have been easy for the son of the story to consider himself as no longer part of the family. He could have been viewed as some sort of second class part of the family or even as a servant, as he had planned. His brother even tried to make a case for some low position for his returning brother.

So he answered and said to his father, 'Lo, these many years I have been serving you; I never transgressed your commandment at any time; and yet you never gave me a young goat, that I might make merry with my friends. But as soon as this son of yours came, who has devoured your livelihood with harlots, you killed the fatted calf for him.'

LUKE 15:29-30 (NKJV)

After we repent, our past will try to return and destroy our life. This is one of the ways the devil works to hinder the working of God in our life. He hates God and does not want anything associated with God to succeed. The devil tries to use any means he can, to stop God's blessing and one very common method is using our past against us.

If we leave the door open, the devil will remind us of all the bad things we have done. He will explain that we are not worthy of receiving the blessings of God. The devil will throw anything he can at us to get us to doubt what God has said. To fight this we need to close the door. We need to say and act on what God has said and done. The past is past! I am now living in the present, in the presence of God and His forgiveness. The past is buried with Jesus and is no longer a part of my life. We must shut the door.

A second area where the closed door is important is dealing with our soul. Our soul includes the mind, will, and emotions, which must be transformed. Too often we are conformed to the ways of the world, we act, think, and talk like the world. It is no wonder that we have problems like the world. To deal with this we must close the door on the worldly input into our soul.

With worldly input closed off, it is easier to receive renewing by the Word of God and to be transformed. By renewing our mind and thinking God's thought after Him, acting as God directs, and speaking about things as God speaks, we are blessed.

> *I beseech you therefore, brethren, by the mercies of God, that you present your bodies a living sacrifice, holy, acceptable to God, which is your reasonable service. And do not be conformed to this world, but be transformed by the renewing of your mind, that you may prove what is that good and acceptable and perfect will of God.*
>
> ROMANS 12:1-2 (NKJV)

Another area of need for the closed door is the wall or hedge around our life. Our heart is much like a field and a good farmer will put a hedge or wall around his field to protect it from attack. The field where the walls are broken down or it has gaps, is opened to many attacks. In the natural, time and effort must be spent protecting the field; the same is true for our heart. The devil is looking for ways to attack Christians and destroy their work and testimony. He is searching for gaps in their hedge.

> *Be sober, be vigilant; because your adversary the devil walks about like a roaring lion, seeking whom he may devour.*
>
> 1 PETER 5:8 (NKJV)

When Jesus was tempted by the devil, Jesus overcame by the Word. Matthew's Gospel mentions that after he had tempted Jesus, the devil left Him, until an opportune time. Christians, with gaps in their hedges, with parts of their wall down, present opportune times to the devil. He is always finding openings through which to attack.

We need to close the door for attacks by filling the gaps and build up our walls. Success in the Christian life requires our dealing with the hedge and wall around our heart. A strong and effective hedge around our heart protects us and gives us opportunities to pray effectively.

Just as it is important to pray for the various aspects of the closed door for our self, it is also important to include prayer for the closed door when we pray for others. The closed door can make the difference between success and failure for people and nations. Without someone praying for the closed door, opportunities will be missed or blocked.

The opportunities of life require open doors of opportunity, they also require a closed door so we are not unable or prohibited from making use of the opportunity. We must keep our past from swamping us, we must keep our soul with all diligence, and we must protect our heart. These protections come from closed doors. It is time to pray for closed doors.

Let us pray!

Article 21

GOOD GOVERNMENT

A round the world there are a variety of political parties and governments. They have a wide range of views as to how to best govern a nation and people. Some parties and governments are good, working to make life better; others seem more interested in gaining or maintaining power (while insisting that they only want power so they can do good things for the country). Some are tyrants, some are dictators, some are benevolent despots, while some are representatives of groups, classes, or the people. Now before you assume too much, I was thinking about the political parties and governments of the time of the Roman Empire. However, things may also be like some of this in your country today.

Governments have been a part of life since the earliest times of man. In Genesis, Chapter 11, we read of an early attempt by men to govern. They set out to build a tower to be the center point of their government. This was a rejection of God. This government made great and wonderful claims; you can almost see the TV advertisement; "This government will be a great government and benefit all mankind". They claimed, as many have claimed, to be part of a change for a new and better government.

And they said, "Come, let us build ourselves a city, and a tower whose top is in the heavens; let us make a name for ourselves, lest we be scattered abroad over the face of the whole earth." But the Lord came down to see the city and the tower which the sons of men had built. And the Lord said, "Indeed the people are one and they all have one language, and this is what they begin to do; now nothing that they propose to do will be withheld from them. Come, let Us go down and there confuse their language, that they may not understand one another's speech." So the Lord scattered them abroad from there over the face of all the earth, and they ceased building the city.

GENESIS 11:4-8 (NKJV)

From that "glorious" beginning, man has worked every idea, plan, and scheme imaginable to find a good government or a way to control people. Throughout history the best laid plans of men have failed; beginning with man's strength, wisdom, and abilities is never enough to overcome the problems of a nation or society. Still, time after time, men have conceived great new plans and convinced people that this new plan was the answer. And while some governments have worked better for people than others, until the future millennial reign of Christ, governments will come and go, all of them based on man bound to struggle or fail.

There have been several responses to this problem of governance. Some people have given up all hope for government. Sometimes this response has been to seek a place and means of hiding from governments and their problems. Others have looked for some form of balance of living under the government, but apart from it. And still others have sought to put controls on governments.

The Bible presents other solutions to the problem of government. The best solution is that which was offered to Israel; let God be the king of the country. This solution makes demands on people; they must follow the rules and commands of God. And most people react to this as Israel did, they reject this solution. They asked to have a king like other nations.

> *Nevertheless the people refused to obey the voice of Samuel; and they said, "No, but we will have a king over us, that we also may be like all the nations, and that our king may judge us and go out before us and fight our battles." And Samuel heard all the words of the people, and he repeated them in the hearing of the Lord. So the Lord said to Samuel, "Heed their voice, and make them a king." And Samuel said to the men of Israel, "Every man go to his city."*
>
> 1 SAMUEL 8:19-22 (NKJV)

The next solution is prayer. And while prayer is not a form of government, prayer is God's solution to making governments work better. He has ordained men and women praying for their government as His means of righting wrongs, fixing failures, and protecting the people. Biblical prayer always has been and still is the fix for man's failure. It does not matter what type of government you must deal with, large or small, good or bad, prayer brings help to the problems and solutions where things seem impossible.

However, there is a big problem with using prayer to fix the problems of governments; Christians must pray. If we sit idly by and let the solutions of man shape our government, then we will reap what we have sown; corruption, destruction, wickedness, deception, and evil. This is not what God planned, nor what He wants. God is seeking a man or woman to stand in the gap for a government and pray.

The people of the land have used oppressions, committed robbery, and mistreated the poor and needy; and they wrongfully oppress the stranger. So I sought for a man among them who would make a wall, and stand in the gap before Me on behalf of the land, that I should not destroy it; but I found no one. Therefore I have poured out My indignation on them; I have consumed them with the fire of My wrath; and I have recompensed their deeds on their own heads," says the Lord God.

 EZEKIEL 22:29-31 (NKJV)

You might say, "That is from the Old Testament." Well okay, but please remember that Paul affirms in his writing that what we call the Old Testament has value for us today and it is God's Word.

All Scripture is given by inspiration of God, and is profitable for doctrine, for reproof, for correction, for instruction in righteousness,

2 TIMOTHY 3:16 (NKJV)

However, here is God's command to pray for our government from the New Testament as well.

Therefore I exhort first of all that supplications, prayers, intercessions, and giving of thanks be made for all men, for kings and all who are in authority, that we may lead a quiet and peaceable life in all godliness and reverence. For this is good and acceptable in the sight of God our Savior, who desires all men to be saved and to come to the knowledge of the truth.

1 TIMOTHY 2:1-4 (NKJV)

Beyond the obvious praying for leaders, we should be praying for the government so men will have the opportunity to be saved and have knowledge of the truth; this is praying for opportunities for the Gospel. These prayers may vary from country to country depending on the political and cultural climate.

In some places, prayers may be needed for a change of the current regulations and standards thus opening the door for evangelism. In other places prayer may be needed for situations that hinder boldness to speak, opening ways to reach people who are otherwise without hope. In other places prayers may be needed for the church to awaken and cause it to stand for the Gospel or prayer may be needed for establishment of new churches. The key is listening to the Holy Spirit as He directs prayers to obtain answers to the needs of the country and people.

Prayer should be ready to deal with the impossible. In many places around the world, and quite possibly in your neighborhood, there are situations that seem impossible. The government cannot solve the problems. The leaders and people may not know what to do; the standard wisdom of the day is not working and nothing seems to help.

However, our God is able to do the seemingly impossible. It is one of His best things! Page after page of the Bible is filled with problems and situations that for the people involved it seemed answers were impossible. The record is clear that time after time God has done things people deemed impossible. He can do that for countries and people today; if we will pray.

We need to be praying for governments and for those people involved in government. Pray that leaders would seek help from God. Pray for the wisdom and good character of those in all levels of government. Pray for people and governments to do what is right and not to cheat the people. And pray for opportunities for the Gospel.

Your standing in the gap for your country, or a country God places on your heart is important. Your prayers are crucial to what happens in a country. Your prayers make a difference for salvation and life. God is looking for a man or woman who will pray for the governments of nations. Can He use you? It is time to pray.

Let us pray!

Article 22

THE CITY OF OUR GOD

G od has blessed me with opportunities to travel and everywhere I go people ask me where I am from. And even though I know what they will say, I always tell them the same thing; "I am from Longmont, Colorado". This always gets a response of, "Where is that?" Then I respond with, "It is near Boulder". People then respond by saying, "Oh, I know Boulder". Although it is not the capital of the United States, or even the capital of Colorado, people everywhere have heard of Boulder. The city of Boulder is famous.

There are many famous cities around the world. These are places that millions of people have heard of and know where it is or at least something about it. These are cities like New York, Los Angeles, Paris, Beijing, Berlin, Innsbruck, Rio de Janeiro and others, each known for its location, an important product or industry, as a political center, cultural hub, or as an important crossroads. Some are famous for good things; others are famous for bad. However, there is one city more famous than all the rest, it is Jerusalem.

And to his son I will give one tribe, that My servant
David may always have a lamp before Me in Jerusalem,

the city which I have chosen for Myself, to put My name there.

1 KINGS 11:36 (NKJV)

Jerusalem is an old city, known to millions of people around the world. The name brings thoughts of reverence and awe for many, and for others it brings anger and hatred. This city has been the center of the greatest kingdom of all time under the rule of kings David and Solomon. It has also been the battleground for many conflicts and wars; for the rulers of the Roman Empire it was a stumbling block to their rule of the Middle East. For thousands of years great nations have fought over it. Politicians have wrangled and battled, this city has had everything, except peace.

However, through all its comings and goings, God has called for prayer for the peace of this city. Today, God continues to call for prayer. He is looking for men and women to pray for this special place, to pray for Jerusalem.

It is important to pray for Jerusalem for many reasons. Chief among these is obedience. There is great power in prayer, but if we will not be obedient to God, we will not experience this power. Without obedience, our prayers are just noise. The willing and obedient are the people who get answers to their prayers.

If you are willing and obedient, You shall eat the good of the land;

ISAIAH 1:19 (NKJV)

If I forget you, O Jerusalem, Let my right hand forget its skill! If I do not remember you, Let my tongue cling to the roof of my mouth—If I do not exalt Jerusalem Above my chief joy.

PSALM 137:5-6 (NKJV)

We also pray for Jerusalem, to repay a great debt. We owe so much to the Jews and what God has done through them. From the Jews we have the Old Testament and examples of great men of faith like Abraham. The city itself came to be a great city for the Jewish nation and the world through the efforts of kings David and Solomon. Jesus was born and raised as a Jew. His life of obedience and faith was impossible except by living in a Jewish family.

> *What shall I render to the Lord For all His benefits toward me?*
>
> PSALM 116:12 (NKJV)

> *It pleased them indeed, and they are their debtors. For if the Gentiles have been partakers of their spiritual things, their duty is also to minister to them in material things.*
>
> ROMANS 15:27 (NKJV)

It is also good to pray for Jerusalem, because it is good for us. It is enlightened self-interest to pray for this city. There is a blessing, God promises prosperity and good, to those who will pray for Jerusalem. When we pray for Jerusalem, God breaks through our problems and brings us His answers and blessings.

> *Pray for the peace of Jerusalem: "May they prosper who love you. Peace be within your walls, Prosperity within your palaces." For the sake of my brethren and companions, I will now say, "Peace be within you." Because of the house of the Lord our God I will seek your good.*
>
> PSALM 122:6-9 (NKJV)

We also pray for Jerusalem, for peace. Just as salvation came from Jerusalem, through the death and resurrection of Jesus, so peace can and will only come from Jerusalem and this peace, the peace of God, is real peace. The Hebrew word for peace is shalom; it speaks of well being, completeness, and welfare. It has been described as "nothing missing, nothing broken". For self, family, and nation to have nothing missing and nothing broken would be great peace.

> *You will arise and have mercy on Zion; For the time to favor her, Yes, the set time, has come. For Your servants take pleasure in her stones, And show favor to her dust. So the nations shall fear the name of the Lord, And all the kings of the earth Your glory. For the Lord shall build up Zion; He shall appear in His glory. He shall regard the prayer of the destitute, And shall not despise their prayer.*
>
> PSALM 102:13-17 (NKJV)

> *I have set watchmen on your walls, O Jerusalem; They shall never hold their peace day or night. You who make mention of the Lord, do not keep silent, And give Him no rest till He establishes And till He makes Jerusalem a praise in the earth.*
>
> ISAIAH 62:6-7 (NKJV)

It is time to pray for the peace of Jerusalem.

Let us pray!

Article 23

BREAKUP
THE FALLOW GROUND

I live in an area that was once called the Great American Desert. This area is so dry that for decades most people believed that farming was impossible; this impeded the settlement of the area for a generation. With improvements in agricultural methods and water use, the area was settled and the land was made fruitful and productive.

The farmer coming to Colorado also found that the ground was very hard, in some places a new type of plow was necessary to break up the ground and make it usable. In other places in America the difficulty was removing the rocks from the soil; there are places where the process of removing the rocks from the fields has continued for several hundred years. Other places the problem was the thick forests, the farmer would work for years removing trees and stumps from the area he wished to cultivate. Whatever the problem the successful farmer, broke up the ground, removed the rocks, pulled the stumps, or whatever was necessary to bring the land under cultivation.

Sow for yourselves righteousness; Reap in mercy; Break
up your fallow ground, For it is time to seek the Lord,
Till He comes and rains righteousness on you.

HOSEA 10:12 (NKJV)

We also need to "breakup the fallow ground." The nations stand before us just as the so called Great American Desert did before the settlers of nearly two hundred years ago. Will we breakup the fallow ground or will we leave the ground unproductive. With regard to the nations will we enter the yoke of Jesus and pray, or will we allow the nations to lay fallow, producing another generation of people lost?

Before us stand the nations, they are fallow ground waiting for preparation, waiting for the sower and reaper. When people have plowed up the land in prayer, when they have broken up the hard ground, the Father has been gracious to shower that land with revival. There are few places where we can see the ground has been prepared and the blessing is pouring in. However, many areas in many nations is still hard ground, the efforts of churches or missionaries are difficult and often thwarted. The problem is a lack of prayer. We have not broken up the fallow ground. We have not joined with Jesus, taken on yoke and burden, and prayed.

One of the keys to success, especially in outreach, is preparation. Often things do not work out well or as expected because of poor preparation. We live in an age that is in such a hurry that preparation has become a lost art. People often act without preparation, they act like, "Do it now, if it fails, go and do something else". Many enterprises never have a chance because there was little, if any preparation to make it work

Look at the preparation for the coming of Jesus. The Old Testament of the Bible is filled with record of the preparation. In prophesies, in psalms, and many other passages, we have a description of the coming event. King David saw the coming the King. Job saw the coming of his

Redeemer. Isaiah saw the healing and delivering One who was wounded for us.

Another example of great preparation is seen in the ministry of Jesus. For three years He prayed and prepared for the Day of Pentecost. Daily He talked with His disciples preparing them for this momentous day. He was constantly in prayer for them, preparing the way for this event. He spoke about it; He taught about it, He prayed about it. He prepared the climate; the people came to have great expectations. Even after it looked like everything had failed, still the 120 disciples stayed in Jerusalem and received the Holy Spirit.

A study of the great revivals of Christian history reveals great preparation as well. Time-after-time the reports of a so called sudden move of God, come after there had been great preparation, often months and years of preparation. In most full reports of a revival we see a powerful ministry of prayer that prepared the way. Men and women worked and prayed until the climate was changed. An area where it was impossible for revival to come changed and then revival came. Spiritual ground so hard nothing could grow; changed, it received the seeds and yielded a great harvest.

A change in conditions does not happen very often. Instead of praying for change, people take a "whatever God will do" attitude and then wonder why nothing happens. God expects His people to prepare for His moves. This is the work of the ministry, the ministry of all the people, the work of prayer. When people pray, not just casually asking for it, but with desperate longing situations change. When people take responsibility to pray for revival, seeking real change to the soil of hearts, then we will have revival.

In the Parable of the Sower we see the difference in types of soil with the corresponding variation in the results of the sowing. There was the wayside, the rocky soil, the thorny area, and the good ground. The good ground produced fruit and good results. The other conditions did not produce fruit.

*But he who received seed on the good ground is he who
hears the word and understands it, who indeed bears
fruit and produces: some a hundredfold, some sixty,
some thirty."*

MATTHEW 13:18-23 (NKJV)

Soil has to be prepared to be good soil. This is the work of the
ministry of prayer. By prayer we can and must prepare the way for
revival. Will you pray? Will you pray for a change of the soil, removal of
rocks and thorns?

If you will pray change can be made in even the most difficult places,
the remote place or the modern city; all can see revival. The question is
will you pray? It is time to pray for revival.

Let us pray!

Article 24

THE LIST

Christmas was always a big event at our house as I was growing up. Along about the end of October and always well before Thanksgiving Day, each of us would begin writing out a list of things we would like as gifts for Christmas. This was our practice as far back as I can remember and it was nice to get everyone's list and be able to think about what you wanted to get them, knowing that these were things they would like. We also learned very early on, that we should put some clothes we like on the list, because we were going to get some clothes and this way we could express our preferences.

Mom was the coordinator, with everyone telling her what they planned to get, so she could steer us away from buying what someone else was buying; with two sisters and two brothers, duplication of gifts could have been a problem. So when we were ready to go shopping we took a list made from the lists of the other family members.

Today I would like to ask you about your list, not for shopping, but for praying. When we read about many of the great men and women of prayer, they kept prayer lists and saw them as an important part of their prayer times and a help to their faith, both by remembering to pray for people and in building up their faith by recording God's wonderful answers to their prayers. I encourage people to use this tool. A good way to do this review is to look at my Christmas shopping list experience.

THE SHOPPING LIST

What was the goal of the shopping list? When I made out a shopping list for my Christmas shopping, I did so as part of a desire to do something nice or good for a family member (even my sisters). If we turn this to prayer, what is the goal of a prayer list? We may have several answers to this question, but let us use the same goal as my shopping list, to do something nice or good for others. Please take note, in shopping I was looking for something the person wanted. In prayer, I should be seeking first the Kingdom of God and His will being done here on earth. This is what people want, even if they do not know it yet. With Kingdom priority, my prayers will seek what truly blesses.

WHO IS ON YOUR LIST?

My shopping list had the names of family members and friends for whom I was buying gifts. Our prayer list should have what God has placed on our heart. Often God will give us opportunities to pray for people and events. We see this in Jesus' prayer ministry; He was constantly confronted by people needing help and seeking His prayers. Sometimes He prayed for them and His faith-filled prayers brought immediate answers. There was no need to place them on a prayer list. This should be the same for us, in some of the opportunities we get for prayer; we should pray and expect to see answers, now. However, there also were times when Jesus prayed as part of His prayer life for people and events far beyond just the moment. For example, Peter was on Jesus' prayer list. And you and I continue to be on His prayer list.

And the Lord said, "Simon, Simon! Indeed, Satan has asked for you, that he may sift you as wheat. But I have prayed for you, that your faith should not fail; and when you have returned to Me, strengthen your brethren."

Luke 22:31-32 (NKJV)

Therefore He is also able to save to the uttermost those who come to God through Him, since He always lives to make intercession for them.

Hebrews 7:25 (NKJV)

WHAT DO THEY WANT?

When I made out my shopping list, I selected items from the list of each member of my family. I listed items they wrote down as the things they wanted. This is important for prayer as well; what do they want. There is often an obvious answer, but many times the answer sought needs clarification before we pray. Sometimes the sought answer is so nebulous that no one knows what they want, such as "Please bless me." And often it is important to clarify, for faith to flow.

So Jesus answered and said to him, "What do you want Me to do for you?" The blind man said to Him, "Rabboni, that I may receive my sight." Then Jesus said to him, "Go your way; your faith has made you well." And immediately he received his sight and followed Jesus on the road.

Mark 10:51-52 (NKJV)

HOW ARE YOU GOING TO GET THE GIFT?

Having the list was great because I knew what people wanted. However, just knowing was not enough; I had to go and get it. So I had to seek the right store (often Mom had an idea where to go to find what I wanted), find the right item, and make the purchase.

Knowing what is wanted is important, but next we need to know God's will and promise. Answers to prayer are by faith and our faith is in God and His promises. The best answers come by knowing God's will and what God has said concerning the need for which we are now seeking an answer. To be effective in prayer, we must know God's will and what He promises and then ask as He directs.

> *Grace and peace be multiplied to you in the knowledge of God and of Jesus our Lord, as His divine power has given to us all things that pertain to life and godliness, through the knowledge of Him who called us by glory and virtue, by which have been given to us exceedingly great and precious promises, that through these you may be partakers of the divine nature, having escaped the corruption that is in the world through lust.*
>
> 2 PETER 1:2-4 (NKJV)

WRAP IT AND PLACE IT UNDER THE TREE

It was one thing to get the gift, but then it had to be wrapped and wrapping is not one of my favorite things. One year I worked this out by having one sister wrap the gift placed in a box, for the other sister!

In prayer, wrapping up the answers and making it available requires three things. First, answers come by faith. When we pray in faith, we believe before we see.

> *Therefore I say to you, whatever things you ask when you pray, believe that you receive them, and you will have them.*
>
> MARK 11:24 (NKJV)

The second requirement is that answers come by good confession. To be successful in prayer we must say what God says. How many times did Abraham state that he was the Father of many nations? That is what the new name God gave him means. So, every time he met with someone, every time he had to state his name, he said "I am the father of many nations" And don't you know that people who knew a little about him looked at him as some kind of kook; "This guy does not have a son, he is too old to have a son." Yet Abraham said what God said, he said it and believed it over the evidence he saw and what others said.

> *And not being weak in faith, he did not consider his own body, already dead (since he was about a hundred years old), and the deadness of Sarah's womb. He did not waver at the promise of God through unbelief, but was strengthened in faith, giving glory to God, and being fully convinced that what He had promised He was also able to perform.*
>
> ROMANS 4:19-21 (NKJV)

Third requirement is that answers come by praise and thanksgiving. We are called to praise God for His answers even before we see them manifest. Praise and thanksgiving before the answer comes is powerful faith in action.

> *Be anxious for nothing, but in everything by prayer and supplication, with thanksgiving, let your requests be made known to God;*
>
> PHILIPPIANS 4:6 (NKJV)

There is great joy in seeing my family members open a gift of something they want. When they were young, my sisters would squeal with delight and I remember, to this day, how great it was to hear their joy with a gift.

Today there are many people on our prayer lists, people who need to have answers to our prayers. They need answer that will make them squeal with delight in what God has done for them. It is time to pray.

> *Then our mouth was filled with laughter, and our tongue with singing. Then they said among the nations, "The Lord has done great things for them." The Lord has done great things for us, and we are glad.*
>
> Psalm 126:2-3 (NKJV)

Let us pray!

Article 25

GO IN AND POSSESS

A s you have read before in the pages of *Voice of Thanksgiving*, I was once a football coach. I coached the defensive players of the high school where I taught classes. One year we played a very good team from the Denver area. In the first half of the game, they scored nearly every time they had the ball, putting up 35 points.

However, as we came off the field there was a feeling among the coaches that something had changed. During the half-time break, we always made a few adjustments based on what we saw the other team doing and this night we did that. Then we gathered to talk with the entire team about what we should do in the second half. We were ready to tell them that things had changed, when the team began to talk about it. Sure we had given up a lot of points; but we had taken the other team's best shot and we were still standing. The team was convinced that something had changed and we could, not just play better, but win the game.

We went out and played well. The offence was great, making long drive after long drive, most of them for a score. The defense played well, stopping the attacks of the other team. With seconds left in the game, we scored a final touchdown to win 36-35!

The same thing happened to Joshua. No he did not play for the Jerusalem Rams or for the Israeli Eagles football teams. He was the new leader of Israel and had been given the task of leading the people in their conquest of the land God had given them. For forty years Israel had wandered in the wilderness, waiting for a generation of doubters to die off. Finally the time had come, finally things had changed; now God was telling Joshua and Israel to go in and possess the Promised Land.

> *Now, O Israel, listen to the statutes and the judgments which I teach you to observe, that you may live, and go in and possess the land which the Lord God of your fathers is giving you.*
>
> DEUTERONOMY 4:1 (NKJV)

Things had not gone well in the first half. God had brought them out of Egypt and through the Red Sea, but when the spies came back with a bad report, doubt, fear, and unbelief, ruled the day and that entire generation would not enter the Promised Land. Only Joshua and Caleb were exceptions to this lack of faith and trust in God. For forty years Israel had wandered in the wilderness. Obviously Israel was not winning; not a single man, woman, or child had entered the Promised Land, not a single acre of land had been taken. But things changed.

Now a new generation began to trust God and was ready to do great exploits. Joshua, Caleb, and the people, were strong in the Lord and knew and trusted in the power of God's great might. They saw the situation, all they faced, armies, cities, walls, and obstacles, through the eye of faith in God. They agreed with God and began to say what He was saying. They walked in obedience to God and His commands. They became a force that could not be stopped and they won, they took the Land!

> *but the people who know their God shall be strong, and carry out great exploits.*
>
> DANIEL 11:32B (NKJV)

It is time for the same thing to happen to us. This generation must trust God and do great exploits. We must be strong in the Lord and know and trust in the power of God's great might. We must see the situation, all that we face, through the eye of faith in God. We must agree with God and say what He is saying. We must walk in obedience to God and His commands. We must pray and be a force that will not be stopped and we must win, and take the land!

In that football game I wrote about in the beginning of this article, at halftime there was a change, the coaches felt it and planned to talk to the team about it, but the players felt it too. So they decided to go out and win the game, and did so!

The game has changed for us as well. The world has expected the demise of the Christian faith for centuries and has not gotten their expectation. The gods of this world, money, power, science, ideas, philosophies, governments, technology, organizations, and the panoply of other gods that were going to meet every need of man, have all failed.

People continue to follow in the wake of these failings because they do not know the score or they do not know where to turn for help. For a long time Christians have stood, like a fighter with his hands down, taking punch after punch, but most of the time we have continued to stand, though battered and bloody. But no more, now is the time for all of this to change.

It is time for us to go in and possess the land. It is time to remove the blinders from the eyes of people so they can see their need for redemption and it sole source, Jesus Christ. It is time to pull down the walls that have held people captive to sin, destruction, and death. It is time to do battle and win!

> *For though we walk in the flesh, we do not war according*
> *to the flesh. For the weapons of our warfare are not*
> *carnal but mighty in God for pulling down strongholds,*

*casting down arguments and every high thing that
exalts itself against the knowledge of God, bringing
every thought into captivity to the obedience of Christ,*

2 CORINTHIANS 10:3-5 (NKJV)

Around the world and in your neighborhood, there are strongholds
that have an ice grip on the people. Pulling down strongholds begins
with prayer. There are arguments thrown about proclaiming this
and that, seeking to dismiss, disdain, and destroy the Christian faith.
Casting down arguments begins with prayer. There are high things that
have exalted themselves over the people, churches, cities, and nations,
proclaiming themselves as king. Casting down high things begins
with prayer. There are thought producing factories throughout the
land, seeking to fill every heart and mind with their dirty, disgusting,
denigrating thoughts. Bringing thoughts into obedience of Christ
begins with prayer.

*Yet in all these things we are more than conquerors
through Him who loved us.*

ROMANS 8:37 (NKJV)

*Now thanks be to God who always leads us in triumph
in Christ, and through us diffuses the fragrance of
His knowledge in every place. For we are to God the
fragrance of Christ among those who are being saved
and among those who are perishing. To the one we are
the aroma of death leading to death, and to the other
the aroma of life leading to life. And who is sufficient
for these things?*

2 CORINTHIANS 2:14-16 (NKJV)

S. D. Gordon writes, "Prayer is striking the winning blow . . . service is gathering up the results." We have much work to do; to the natural eye the score looks hopeless. It seems the world must win, but we do not look by the natural eye, but by the spiritual. Our work has waited long enough, it is time to pray, work, and win. Things have changed, it is time to go in and possess the land. It is time to pray.

Let us pray!

Prayer For Salvation

Troubles, troubles, troubles, the world is filled with difficult situations. It is easy to be overcome by fear or even terror. Every day is a battle. The Bible reveals that there would be times like these. It also explains that there is an answer. The answer to our troubles is making Jesus Christ Lord over our life.

Now is the time to get to know Him and the Bible explains what we need to do. If you believe in your heart what these verses say, you can be saved. Read the verse and then pray the prayer. Pray trusting God to save you and give you eternal life.

> *If you confess with your mouth the Lord Jesus and believe in your heart that God has raised Him from the dead, you will be saved. For with the heart one believes unto righteousness, and with the mouth confession is made unto salvation.*
>
> Romans 10:9-10 (NKJV)

Dear God in Heaven, I recognize that I am a sinner, and I need help. I believe that Jesus is your Son. I believe that He died on the cross for my sins and that you raised Him from the dead. I receive Jesus now and make Him the Lord of my life.

Jesus come to me, I welcome you as my Lord and Savior. Father, I believe that I am now saved. I confess with my mouth that I am saved and born again. I am now a child of God.

Congratulations you are now part of the body of Christ!

Now that you are a Christian, you should build a new life with Jesus Christ and other Christians. It would be good to:

Tell someone of your decision (you could email me at dave@voiceofthanksgiving.com).

Get a Bible and read it.

Find a Christian church that believes the Bible, be an active and faithful participant at meetings.

Get baptized.

Learn to pray, effective prayers that avail much.

A Few Selected Books on Prayer

Bounds, E. M. *The Complete Works of E. M. Bounds on Prayer*

Bevington, G. C. *Remarkable Miracles*

Carre, E.G. Captain, Ed. *Praying Hyde—The Life of John "Praying" Hyde*

Cho, Paul Y. *Prayer: Key to Revival*

Copeland, Kenneth. *Prayer Your Foundation for Success*

Dorsett, Lyle Wesley. *E. M. Bounds—Man of Prayer*

Duewel, Wesley. *Mighty Prevailing Prayer*

Duewel, Wesley. *Revival Fire*

Duewel, Wesley. *Touch the World through Prayer*

Eastman, Dick. *The Hour that Changes the World*

Edwards, Jonathan, ed. *The Life and Diary of David Brainerd*

Finney, Charles. *Lectures on Revival*

Finney, Charles. *The Memoirs of Charles G. Finney*

Gordon, S. D. *Quiet Talks on Prayer*

Grubb, Norman. *Rees Howells Intercessor*

Hagin, Kenneth. *Prevailing Prayer to Peace*

Hayford, Jack W. *Prayer is Invading the Impossible*

Lea, Larry, *Could You Not Tarry One Hour?*

Lindsay, Gordon. *Praying to Change the World*

McBirnie, William Steuart. *The Principles of Powerful Prayer*

Miller, Basil. *George Muller*

Miller, Basil. *Praying Hyde*

Müller, George. *Autobiography of George Muller, or A Million and A Half in Answer to Prayer*

Murray, Andrew. *The Believer's Prayer Life*

Murray, Andrew. *The Ministry of Intercessory Prayer*

Murray, Andrew. *With Christ in the School of Prayer*

Nee, Watchman. *The Prayer Ministry of the Church*

Prince, Derek. *Secrets of a Prayer Warrior*

Prince, Derek. *Shaping History through Prayer and Fasting*

Ravenhill, Leonard. *Revival God's Way*

Ravenhill, Leonard. *Why Revival Tarries*

Savelle, Jerry. *Prayer of Petition—Breaking Through the Impossible*

Spencer, Mark D. *The Challenge—Victorious Living in Another Kingdom*

Spencer, Mark D. *A Portrait of Intercession*

Wallis, Arthur. *God's Chosen Fast*

Wallis, Arthur. *In The Day of Thy Power*

Wallis, Arthur. *Pray in the Spirit*

THE BOOK SERIES AND NEWSLETTER

Time to Pray is the fifth volume of the series *Prayer: A Force that Causes Change*. Each book is a collection of articles originally published in the online newsletter *Voice of Thanksgiving*. These articles are presented for developing a powerful prayer life and as a call to effective, prayer that avails much. To purchase copies of these books go to http:// voiceofthanksgiving.com/Book/Book.htm

> *Prayer: A Force that Causes Change*
> VOLUME 1—A CALL TO PRAYER
> VOLUME 2—A LIFE OF PRAYER
> VOLUME 3—FAITHFUL IN PRAYER
> VOLUME 4—EFFECTIVE PRAYER
> VOLUME 5—TIME TO PRAY

Voice of Thanksgiving is a newsletter calling men and women to effective prayer. The *Voice of Thanksgiving* website can be seen at: http:// voiceofthanksgiving.com. You can receive *Voice of Thanksgiving* weekly by email, send an e-mail with the word JOIN in the subject line to: david@voiceofthanksgiving.com.